MALAGA

COMPREHENSIVE GUIDE 2025

A Journey Through Culture, Hidden Gems, Cuisine and Local Secrets in Southern Iberia on the Costa del Sol, Spain – Packed with Detailed Maps & Itinerary Planner

BY

JAMES W. PATRICK

Copyright © 2024 by James W. Patrick. All rights reserved. The content of this work, including but not limited to text, images, and other media, is owned by James W. Patrick and is protected under copyright laws and international agreements. No part of this work may be reproduced, shared, or transmitted in any form or by any means without the explicit written consent of James W. Patrick. Unauthorized use, duplication, or distribution of this material may lead to legal action, including both civil and criminal penalties. For permission requests or further inquiries, please reach out to the author via the contact details provided in the book or on the author's official page.

TABLE OF CONTENTS

Copyright...1
My Experience in Malaga..5
Benefits of this Guide..7

Chapter 1: Introduction to Malaga..10
1.1 Welcome to Malaga...10
1.2 History and Culture...11
1.3 Geography and Climate..12
1.4 Getting to Malaga...14
1.5 Malaga for First Time Travelers...16

Chapter 2: Accommodation Options...18
2.1 Luxury Hotels and Resorts...19
2.2 Budget-Friendly Options..20
2.3 Vacation Rentals and Apartments..22
2.4 Camping in Malaga..23
2.6 Boutique Hotels..24
2.7 Unique Stays: Historic Buildings and Beachfront Properties...........25

Chapter 3: Transportation..27
3.1 Getting Around Malaga..27
3.2 Public Transportation Options...28
3.3 Car Rentals and Driving Tips...29
3.4 Walking and Cycling in Malaga...30
3.5 Boat Tours and Water Sports..33

Chapter 4: Top 10 Attractions & Hidden Gems..36
4.1 Alcazaba Fortress...37
4.2 Gibralfaro Castle..39
4.3 Malaga Cathedral...41

4.4 Picasso Museum...43
4.5 Caminito del Rey...44
4.6 Nerja Caves...46
4.7 La Malagueta Beach..48
4.8 Mercado de Atarazanas...50
4.9 El Palo Neighborhood...51
4.10 Mijas Pueblo..53
4.11 Outdoor Activities and Adventures...54
4.12 Guided Tours and Recommended Tour Operators..56

Chapter 5 Practical Information and Guidance..58
5.1 Maps and Navigation..58
5.2 Five Days Itinerary..60
5.3 Essential Packing List...63
5.4 Setting Your Travel Budget...65
5.5 Visa Requirements and Entry Procedures..67
5.6 Safety Tips and Emergency Contacts...69
5.7 Currency Exchange and Banking Services..71
5.8 Language, Communication and Useful Phrases..73
5.9 Shopping in Malaga..75
5.10 Health and Wellness Centers..77
5.11 Useful Websites, Mobile Apps and Online Resources.................................79
5.12 Internet Access and Connectivity...80
5.13 Visitor Centers and Tourist Assistance...82

Chapter 6: Gastronomic Delights..85
6.1 Dining Options and Top Restaurants..85
6.2 Traditional Andalusian Cuisine..88
6.3 Tapas and Wine Bars..90
6.4 Cooking Classes and Culinary Tours...93
6.5 Local Markets and Street Food..95
8.6 Nightlife and Flamenco Shows..97

Chapter 7: Day Trips and Excursions 100
7.1 Granada 101
7.2 Seville 103
7.3 Cordoba 106
7.4 Ronda 107

Chapter 8: Events and Festivals 110
8.1 Malaga Fair 110
8.2 Holy Week 113
8.3 Malaga Film Festival 116
8.4 Jazz Festival 118
8.5 Christmas in Malaga 121
Insider Tips and Recommendations 125

MY EXPERIENCE IN MALAGA

Arriving in Málaga felt like stepping into a sunlit dream. The Mediterranean breeze greeted me warmly as I left the airport, instantly melting away the stresses of travel. Málaga, with its golden streets and vibrant energy, enveloped me in a sense of relaxation and wonder. The city, perched on Spain's Costa del Sol, radiates charm and invites exploration. As I wandered through its streets, I was struck by a seamless blend of history, culture, and coastal beauty that made each moment memorable. My journey began with a deep dive into Málaga's rich historical tapestry. The Alcazaba, a Moorish fortress that towers over the city, was a highlight of my visit. Walking through its ancient walls and lush gardens, I could almost hear the echoes of its storied past. The panoramic views from the Alcazaba were breathtaking, offering a sweeping vista of Málaga and the sparkling Mediterranean Sea. Adjacent to the Alcazaba, the Roman Theatre stood as a poignant reminder of the city's layered history. The contrast between the Roman ruins and the Moorish fortress underscored Málaga's cultural evolution through the ages, creating a vivid historical narrative that I was eager to explore further.

Art, too, plays a central role in Málaga's identity. A visit to the Picasso Museum was a pilgrimage of sorts for me, given that Pablo Picasso was born in this city. The museum, housed in a beautifully restored 17th-century palace, offered a profound insight into Picasso's artistic journey. The collection, spanning his entire career, allowed me to witness the evolution of his style and vision. Each piece told a story, and the museum's intimate setting made it easy to appreciate the nuances of Picasso's work. Equally captivating was the Carmen Thyssen Museum, which showcased an impressive array of 19th-century Spanish paintings. The museum's cozy ambiance enhanced my experience, allowing me to lose myself in the intricate details and emotions of each artwork. Málaga's culinary scene is another treasure trove of experiences. The local cuisine, with its emphasis on fresh, local ingredients, was a revelation. Dining at a lively tapas bar was a feast for the senses. The vibrant atmosphere, filled with the sounds of clinking glasses and lively conversations, was as enjoyable as the food. Each tapa, from the succulent gambas al pil-pil to the crispy croquetas, was a testament to the region's culinary expertise. The flavors were bold and satisfying, and the communal dining experience provided a genuine taste of Málaga's food culture.

No visit to Málaga would be complete without experiencing its coastal allure. La Malagueta Beach, with its inviting sands and clear waters, offered a perfect escape for relaxation. Spending a day on the beach, basking in the warmth of the sun and listening to the gentle waves, was a highlight of my trip. The Paseo Marítimo, the promenade that stretches along the coastline, was another favorite spot. Strolling along this scenic route, with the sea on one side and charming cafes on the other, was a delightful way to soak in the city's coastal beauty. The sunset views from the promenade were particularly enchanting, casting a warm, pink glow over the city and creating a picturesque backdrop for reflection. Málaga's vibrant cultural scene extends beyond its museums and beaches. During my visit, I was fortunate enough to experience the Feria de Agosto, a week-long festival that transforms the city into a lively celebration of music, dance, and food. The streets came alive with the rhythms of flamenco, and the energy of the festival was infectious. Participating in the festivities, surrounded by locals and fellow travelers, offered a glimpse into Málaga's communal spirit and traditions.

As my time in Málaga drew to a close, I felt a mixture of sadness and gratitude. The city had embraced me with open arms, offering a rich tapestry of experiences that were both enriching and enchanting. Leaving Málaga, I carried with me a sense of having discovered a place that feels timeless yet vibrantly alive. Málaga invites you to linger, to immerse yourself in its history, art, and natural beauty. It promises not just a visit but an experience that lingers in your heart long after you've left. For anyone seeking a destination where the past and present converge in a sunlit embrace, Málaga is ready to share its magic.

BENEFITS OF THIS GUIDE

This guide is meticulously designed to be your ultimate companion for discovering the city's myriad attractions. Whether you're wandering through its historic streets, indulging in local culinary delights, or embarking on adventurous excursions, this guide provides all the essential information to ensure a memorable visit. From navigating the city's dynamic landscape to uncovering hidden gems, this guide will equip you with the knowledge needed to fully immerse yourself in the charm and allure of Malaga.

Maps and Navigation: Effective navigation is key to unlocking the full experience of Malaga, and our guide provides comprehensive tools to help you traverse the city with ease. Featuring detailed printed maps, you'll find clear layouts of central Malaga, historic neighborhoods, and essential landmarks, designed to be both functional and user-friendly. For those who prefer digital assistance, we've included interactive maps accessible via links and QR codes. These digital resources offer real-time updates and enhanced details on local amenities and public transportation routes, ensuring that you can effortlessly navigate both well-trodden paths and off-the-beaten-track areas.

Accommodation Options: Malaga's diverse accommodation landscape caters to every traveler's needs, whether you're seeking luxury or budget-friendly options. Our guide delves into high-end hotels that offer indulgent comforts and panoramic views of the Mediterranean, perfect for those looking to splurge. For a more intimate experience, boutique hotels are highlighted, providing unique character and personalized service. Budget-conscious travelers will find recommendations for affordable hostels and guesthouses that do not compromise on comfort or convenience. Additionally, we cover vacation rentals, ideal for families or groups who desire a home-like setting during their stay, complete with details on locations, amenities, and pricing.

Transportation: Navigating Malaga is straightforward with its well-organized transportation network, and our guide provides in-depth coverage of all available options. Public transportation, including buses, trains, and the metro system, is efficiently mapped out with timetables and fare information to help you get around the city and its environs. For those opting for taxis or ride-sharing services, details on how to access these modes of transport are included. If you prefer the flexibility of driving, our guide offers comprehensive information on car rental services, including key locations and pricing. Additionally, Malaga's pedestrian-friendly areas and cycling paths are detailed for those who wish to explore at a leisurely pace.

Top Attractions: Malaga's rich array of attractions offers something for every type of traveler, and our guide presents an in-depth look at the city's must-see sites. The Picasso Museum stands out, showcasing the life and works of Malaga's most famous artist, while the Alcazaba, a well-preserved Moorish fortress, provides fascinating historical insights and stunning city views. Gibralfaro Castle, perched on a hill, offers panoramic vistas that are both breathtaking and historically significant. The Malaga Cathedral, with its incomplete tower, is a Renaissance marvel that adds to the city's architectural splendor. The Roman Theatre, another gem, gives visitors a glimpse into the ancient past of Malaga, enriching your understanding of its historical landscape.

Practical Information and Travel Resources: For a smooth and hassle-free visit, our guide includes a wealth of practical information and travel resources. It provides essential details on visa and entry requirements, ensuring international travelers are well-prepared for their journey. Emergency contacts are prominently listed, offering quick access to medical, police, and consular services. To facilitate communication, basic Spanish phrases and language tips are included, helping you engage more easily with locals. Additionally, health and safety tips are provided to ensure your well-being, including local safety advice and necessary vaccinations, so you can focus on enjoying your trip.

Culinary Delights: Malaga's culinary scene is a vibrant fusion of traditional Andalusian flavors and modern gastronomy, and our guide offers a tantalizing exploration of its food culture. From savoring espetos (grilled sardines) and refreshing gazpacho to indulging in flavorful paella, we highlight the must-try dishes that define the local cuisine. The guide also covers bustling food markets, such as the Mercado de Atarazanas, where you can sample fresh produce and gourmet delights. For those seeking fine dining experiences, top restaurants offering both local and international cuisine are featured, providing a range of options to suit every palate.

Culture and Heritage: Malaga's rich cultural tapestry is vividly illustrated in its festivals, museums, and historic sites, and our guide delves into these elements with great detail. The city's vibrant festivals, including Semana Santa and Feria de Agosto, offer immersive experiences into local traditions and celebrations. Cultural institutions like the Centre Pompidou Malaga and the Carmen Thyssen Museum provide further insight into the city's artistic heritage. Historic landmarks, such as the old city walls and traditional neighborhoods, are explored, giving visitors a deep understanding of Malaga's past and its evolution into the lively city it is today.

Outdoor Activities and Adventures: For those who thrive in the great outdoors, Malaga presents a wealth of activities that promise adventure and relaxation. The city's beautiful beaches, such as Playa de la Malagueta and Playa de Pedregalejo, are perfect for sunbathing and swimming. Nearby natural parks and hiking trails, including Montes de Malaga Natural Park, offer scenic routes for nature enthusiasts. Water sports enthusiasts will find opportunities for kayaking, sailing, and snorkeling along the stunning coast. Our guide details these activities, providing everything you need to plan an exhilarating outdoor experience.

Shopping: Malaga's shopping scene caters to a variety of tastes and budgets, and our guide provides a comprehensive overview of the best shopping experiences. High street shops on Calle Larios offer a mix of international brands and local boutiques, ideal for those seeking fashionable finds. Souvenir stores and markets provide unique mementos and local crafts, perfect for taking a piece of Malaga home with you. For luxury shoppers, exclusive designer boutiques offer high-end fashion and accessories. Each shopping destination is detailed with insights into what you can expect and where to find the best deals.

Day Trips and Excursions: Beyond the city limits, Malaga serves as a gateway to a variety of exciting day trips and excursions. Our guide highlights destinations such as Ronda, with its dramatic cliffs and historic bridges, and Granada, known for the stunning Alhambra Palace and vibrant cultural scene. The charming coastal town of Nerja, with its famous caves, is also featured as a must-visit spot. Each recommended day trip is described with details on what to see and do, allowing you to expand your exploration beyond Malaga and experience the diverse beauty of southern Spain.

Entertainment and Nightlife: As the sun sets, Malaga transforms into a lively hub of entertainment and nightlife, and our guide covers the best venues to experience this vibrant side of the city. Theaters and live music venues, such as Teatro Cervantes, offer a range of performances from drama to concerts.

CHAPTER 1
INTRODUCTION TO MALAGA

1.1 Welcome to Malaga

Welcome to Málaga, a city where the essence of the Mediterranean pulses through every street and alleyway, offering an experience as vibrant and diverse as its history. Situated on the southern coast of Spain, Málaga embraces visitors with its warm climate, picturesque beaches, and a charm that beckons exploration. From the moment you step into the heart of the city, you'll find yourself immersed in a blend of tradition and modernity that defines Málaga's unique character. Begin your journey at the waterfront, where the sparkling waters of the Mediterranean Sea kiss the golden sands of Playa de La Malagueta. This beach, located just a short walk from the city center, is not merely a place for sunbathing but a lively hub where locals and tourists gather to enjoy the sea breeze and the lively atmosphere. As you stroll along the promenade, you'll encounter a host of cafes and tapas bars offering a taste of Andalusian cuisine and the chance to savor the local delicacies while taking in views of the serene ocean.

The city's historical essence is palpable as you move towards the Alcazaba, a Moorish fortress that stands as a testament to Málaga's rich past. Perched on a hill, this ancient stronghold provides panoramic views of the city and the surrounding landscape, inviting you to reflect on the layers of history that have shaped Málaga. Adjacent to the Alcazaba, you'll find the Roman Theatre, an archaeological treasure that offers a glimpse into the city's Roman heritage. Wander further into the city and you'll discover the Picasso Museum, a celebration of Málaga's most famous son. Situated in the Palacio de Buenavista, the museum showcases an extensive collection of works by Pablo Picasso, offering insight into the artistic evolution of one of the 20th century's most influential artists. Just a short distance away, the Cathedral of Málaga stands with its impressive Renaissance architecture, often referred to as 'La Manquita' due to its incomplete second tower, adding to its intriguing character.

Málaga's vibrant atmosphere extends into its bustling markets and shopping streets. The Atarazanas Market, housed in a former shipyard building, is a sensory delight, offering an array of fresh produce, local specialties, and a glimpse into daily life in Málaga. The surrounding shopping districts invite you to explore boutiques, traditional stores, and modern retail spaces, reflecting the city's blend of historical charm and contemporary flair. In Málaga, every corner tells a story, every street offers a new discovery, and every moment is an opportunity to experience the city's warm hospitality. As you wander through its streets and soak in its rich cultural tapestry, you'll find that Málaga is not just a destination but a journey into the heart of Andalusia.

1.2 History and Culture
Málaga's rich history and culture weaves together a narrative that spans thousands of years, shaped by the many civilizations that have called this vibrant city home. Situated on the southern coast of Spain, Málaga's origins trace back to the Phoenicians, who established it as a trading post around 770 BC. This early settlement laid the foundation for a city that would evolve through successive waves of cultural and historical influence. During the Roman era, Málaga flourished as a prominent port city under the name Malaka. The remnants of this period can still be seen today, with the Roman Theatre standing as a testament to the city's ancient heritage. This well-preserved structure, discovered in the 1950s, offers a glimpse into Málaga's role as a center of cultural and civic life in Roman Hispania.

The fall of the Roman Empire gave way to the Visigoths, who briefly ruled the city before the arrival of the Moors in the 8th century. Under Muslim rule,

Málaga experienced a golden age, marked by the construction of the Alcazaba and the expansion of its fortifications. This period also saw the establishment of the city's cultural and intellectual life, with the Moors leaving an indelible mark on Málaga's architecture and urban design. The Reconquista in the late 15th century brought significant changes to Málaga as it was incorporated into the Kingdom of Castile. The Catholic Monarchs, Ferdinand and Isabella, played a crucial role in this transition, and their influence is evident in the city's Christian monuments and the re-purposing of Moorish structures. The Malaga Cathedral, often referred to as 'La Manquita,' is a striking example of the city's Renaissance period, embodying the architectural ambition of the time.

The 19th and 20th centuries introduced a new chapter in Málaga's story, with industrialization and modernization transforming the city into a dynamic urban center. This era also saw the rise of Málaga's most famous son, Pablo Picasso, whose legacy is celebrated through the Picasso Museum. His innovative contributions to art have cemented Málaga's place on the global cultural map, adding a contemporary dimension to its historical narrative. Today, Málaga stands as a city where ancient history meets modern vibrancy. Its museums, historic sites, and cultural festivals reflect a deep appreciation for its diverse heritage, inviting visitors to delve into its past while enjoying its lively present. The city's evolution through the ages has forged a unique character that continues to captivate and inspire those who come to experience its rich cultural tapestry.

1.3 Geography and Climate

The city's topography includes a series of gentle hills and valleys that contribute to its distinct landscape. Málaga's geography is characterized by its stunning coastal stretch, with picturesque beaches such as Playa de La Malagueta lying within easy reach of the city center. The surrounding mountains provide a dramatic backdrop, adding to the city's visual appeal and offering opportunities for outdoor activities such as hiking and exploring nature.

Climate Overview

Málaga enjoys a Mediterranean climate, characterized by hot, dry summers and mild, wet winters. This climate is one of the city's most appealing features, contributing to its reputation as a year-round destination. The weather in Málaga is generally pleasant, making it an attractive spot for travelers seeking to escape harsher climates.

Spring: Spring, from March to May, is one of the most favorable times to visit Málaga. During these months, the weather is pleasantly warm but not overly hot, with temperatures typically ranging between 15°C and 25°C (59°F to 77°F). The city comes alive with blooming flowers and vibrant greenery, providing a beautiful setting for sightseeing and outdoor activities. Spring is an excellent time for exploring Málaga's historic sites, enjoying the beaches, and attending local festivals such as the Semana Santa (Holy Week) and the Feria de Abril.

Autumn: Autumn, from September to November, offers similarly mild and enjoyable weather. Temperatures during this period range from 17°C to 27°C (63°F to 81°F). The summer crowds have thinned, making it easier to explore popular attractions like the Alcazaba and the Picasso Museum without the bustle of peak tourist season. The autumn months also bring a cultural richness, with various local events and festivals providing opportunities to experience the city's vibrant atmosphere.

Summer: Summer, spanning from June to August, is the peak tourist season in Málaga. During this time, temperatures frequently soar above 30°C (86°F), with July and August often experiencing the highest temperatures. The warm, sunny weather is ideal for beachgoers, with Málaga's coastline offering ample opportunities for sunbathing and water sports. However, the heat can be intense, especially in the city center, so visitors should stay hydrated and seek shade during the hottest parts of the day. Summer is also a lively time in Málaga, with numerous festivals and outdoor events enhancing the city's energetic vibe. The Feria de Málaga in August, for instance, is a highlight of the summer, featuring music, dancing, and traditional celebrations.

Winter: Winter, from December to February, is the least crowded period in Málaga, offering a quieter experience. Temperatures during winter are mild compared to much of Europe, typically ranging between 8°C and 18°C (46°F to 64°F). While the weather is generally mild, occasional rain showers and cooler temperatures can occur. Winter is a good time for those who prefer to avoid large crowds and still enjoy relatively mild weather. The winter months are also ideal for exploring the city's cultural attractions at a more leisurely pace, as well as experiencing the festive Christmas lights and seasonal events that add a special charm to the city.

Navigating Málaga: Navigating Málaga is relatively straightforward due to its compact and accessible layout. The city center is pedestrian-friendly, making it easy to explore on foot. For longer distances, public transportation options such as buses and taxis are readily available. The Málaga Metro, which connects various parts of the city, including the airport, is a convenient option for travelers. Additionally, renting a bicycle or using ride-sharing services can provide a flexible way to get around. Overall, Málaga's geography and climate make it a desirable destination throughout the year. Each season offers its own unique appeal, from the spring and autumn's mild temperatures to the summer's vibrant atmosphere and the winter's serene charm. By understanding the city's climate and seasonal variations, visitors can plan their trip to align with their preferences, ensuring an enjoyable and memorable experience in this captivating Andalusian gem.

1.4 Getting to Malaga

Málaga is well-connected through various modes of transport, making it accessible for travelers from around the globe. Whether you prefer the convenience of air travel, the scenic allure of train journeys, or the flexibility of driving, Málaga offers multiple ways to reach this enchanting city. Here's a comprehensive guide to getting to Málaga, including details on airlines, train services, and road travel, along with useful websites to help you plan your journey.

Air Travel: For most travelers, flying to Málaga is the most efficient and straightforward option. Málaga-Costa del Sol Airport (AGP) serves as the primary international gateway to the city, located just 8 kilometers (5 miles) from the city center. This well-equipped airport connects Málaga with major cities across Europe and beyond, ensuring easy access for international visitors. Several airlines offer flights to Málaga, catering to a range of preferences and budgets. Major European carriers such as Lufthansa (www.lufthansa.com), British Airways (www.britishairways.com), and Air France (www.airfrance.com) provide regular flights from their hubs. For those seeking more economical options, low-cost airlines like Ryanair (www.ryanair.com), EasyJet (www.easyjet.com), and Vueling (www.vueling.com) offer competitive prices and frequent services. North American travelers can find direct flights with airlines such as American Airlines (www.aa.com) and Delta (www.delta.com), especially during peak travel seasons.

Ticket prices vary depending on the season, booking time, and airline. Generally, fares from major European cities range from €100 to €300 for a round-trip ticket, while flights from North America can cost between $500 and $1,200. To find the best deals, utilize flight comparison websites like Skyscanner (www.skyscanner.net) or Google Flights (www.google.com/flights). These platforms allow you to compare prices, view flight schedules, and book tickets directly. Booking a flight is straightforward. Tickets can be purchased through the airline's website or through online travel agencies like Expedia (www.expedia.com) and Booking.com (www.booking.com). Upon arrival at Málaga Airport, travelers can easily reach the city center by taxi, airport shuttle, or rental car, all readily available at the airport.

Train Travel: For those who prefer a more scenic and relaxed mode of travel, trains offer a comfortable and enjoyable way to reach Málaga. The city is well-served by Spain's high-speed rail network, operated by Renfe (www.renfe.com). Renfe's AVE (Alta Velocidad Española) trains connect Málaga with major cities such as Madrid and Barcelona, providing a swift and pleasant journey. The high-speed AVE trains from Madrid to Málaga typically take around 2.5 hours, while the journey from Barcelona lasts about 5.5 hours. The trains are known for their modern amenities and comfortable seating, making the ride both efficient and enjoyable. Ticket prices for AVE trains vary based on the class of service and how far in advance tickets are booked. One-way fares from Madrid generally range from €60 to €150, and from Barcelona, they range from €100 to €200. To secure the best fares, it is advisable to book tickets in advance through the Renfe website or at train stations. The Málaga train station, conveniently located close to the city center, provides easy access to local transportation options, including buses and taxis, facilitating a smooth transition to your final destination.

Road Travel: Driving to Málaga offers the advantage of flexibility and the opportunity to explore the scenic beauty of southern Spain. The city is accessible via major highways such as the A-7 and AP-7, which connect Málaga to various parts of Spain. For those traveling from Madrid, the drive takes approximately 5 to 6 hours, while the journey from Barcelona spans around 10 to 12 hours. International travelers can also reach Málaga by car from neighboring countries, such as France, via the E-15 and E-40 highways. Renting a car is a viable option for visitors who wish to explore the city and its surroundings at their own pace.

Planning Your Arrival: Regardless of the mode of travel you choose, Málaga's well-developed transportation infrastructure ensures a seamless arrival experience. From the convenience of flying to the scenic pleasures of train travel and the flexibility of driving, each option offers a unique way to start your journey in this captivating Andalusian city. By utilizing the available resources and planning your travel in advance, you can ensure a smooth and enjoyable arrival in Málaga, setting the stage for a memorable visit to this vibrant and historic destination.

1.5 Malaga for First Time Travelers

By following these tips, first-time travelers to Málaga will find themselves well-equipped to explore the city's rich cultural landscape, enjoy its culinary delights, and immerse themselves in its historical and social fabric. Each experience will contribute to a memorable journey, making Málaga a city you'll cherish long after you've departed.

Embrace the Local Culinary Scene: Málaga's culinary scene is a vibrant tapestry of flavors and traditions that invites exploration. For first-time visitors, diving into the city's tapas culture is a must. Tapas bars like El Pimpi, located in the heart of the city, offer an authentic taste of Andalusian cuisine. Here, you can enjoy a variety of small dishes, from succulent Iberian ham to freshly made gazpacho, paired with local wines and sherries. To truly experience Málaga's gastronomic offerings, a visit to the Atarazanas Market is highly recommended. This bustling market, housed in a historic building, showcases an array of fresh produce, seafood, and regional delicacies that capture the essence of Andalusian flavor.

Navigating the City with Ease: Málaga's compact layout makes it a pedestrian-friendly city, ideal for exploring on foot. The city center is easily navigable, allowing you to discover its charming streets and hidden gems at your own pace. For those who prefer public transportation, Málaga offers an efficient bus network and reliable taxi services. To streamline your sightseeing, consider purchasing a Málaga City Pass. This pass provides discounted entry to popular attractions, such as the Alcazaba and the Picasso Museum, and helps you avoid long lines. Additionally, the pass includes public transportation options, making it a convenient choice for first-time visitors.

Explore Historical Landmarks: Málaga is rich in historical landmarks that offer a glimpse into its storied past. The Alcazaba, a well-preserved Moorish fortress, stands as a testament to the city's medieval heritage. Located on a hill overlooking the city, it provides panoramic views and a fascinating exploration of ancient architecture. Adjacent to the Alcazaba, the Roman Theatre offers insight into Málaga's Roman era with its well-maintained ruins. For art enthusiasts, the Picasso Museum, situated in the Palacio de Buenavista, showcases the works of Pablo Picasso, providing an invaluable perspective on the city's artistic legacy.

Understand Local Customs and Etiquette: Experiencing Málaga's local customs can enhance your visit and help you connect with the local culture. Spaniards typically enjoy a late dinner, often starting around 9 PM. Embracing this practice by dining at local restaurants during these hours allows you to experience the city's social rhythms and culinary traditions. Additionally, learning a few basic Spanish phrases can significantly improve your interactions with locals and demonstrate your appreciation for their culture. Simple greetings and expressions of gratitude go a long way in making your visit more enjoyable.

Experience Local Festivals and Cultural Events: Málaga's vibrant cultural scene comes alive during its numerous festivals and events throughout the year. The Feria de Málaga, held every August, is a highlight of the city's festival calendar. This lively event features music, dance, and traditional festivities, offering a deep dive into Andalusian culture. Participating in local festivals provides an opportunity to engage with Málaga's traditions and immerse yourself in its celebratory spirit. Keep an eye on the city's event calendar to catch other cultural happenings during your visit, ensuring a richer and more immersive experience.

CHAPTER 2
ACCOMMODATION OPTIONS

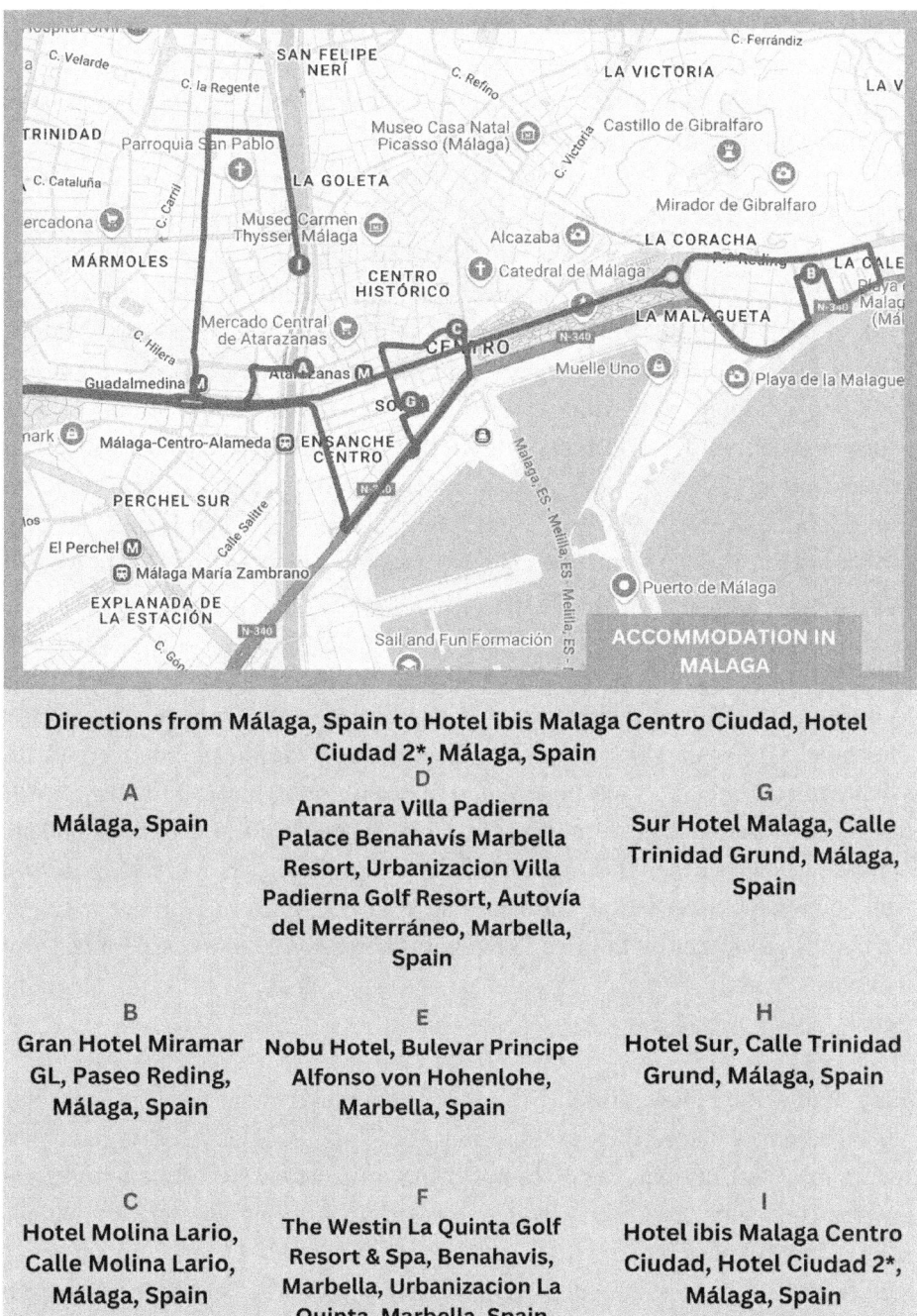

Directions from Málaga, Spain to Hotel ibis Malaga Centro Ciudad, Hotel Ciudad 2*, Málaga, Spain

A Málaga, Spain	**D** Anantara Villa Padierna Palace Benahavís Marbella Resort, Urbanizacion Villa Padierna Golf Resort, Autovía del Mediterráneo, Marbella, Spain	**G** Sur Hotel Malaga, Calle Trinidad Grund, Málaga, Spain
B Gran Hotel Miramar GL, Paseo Reding, Málaga, Spain	**E** Nobu Hotel, Bulevar Principe Alfonso von Hohenlohe, Marbella, Spain	**H** Hotel Sur, Calle Trinidad Grund, Málaga, Spain
C Hotel Molina Lario, Calle Molina Lario, Málaga, Spain	**F** The Westin La Quinta Golf Resort & Spa, Benahavis, Marbella, Urbanizacion La Quinta, Marbella, Spain	**I** Hotel ibis Malaga Centro Ciudad, Hotel Ciudad 2*, Málaga, Spain

2.1 Luxury Hotels and Resorts

When it comes to indulgent getaways in Malaga, the city offers a selection of luxury hotels and resorts that redefine sophistication and comfort. Each establishment promises an extraordinary experience, combining exquisite accommodations with exceptional service and top-notch amenities. Whether you're seeking a serene retreat or a lavish urban experience, Malaga's luxury accommodations cater to every whim.

Gran Hotel Miramar: Situated along Malaga's sunlit coastline, Gran Hotel Miramar is an emblem of elegance. This five-star establishment, housed in a historic building that once served as a royal palace, blends classic grandeur with modern luxury. Guests can expect rooms adorned with sumptuous fabrics and state-of-the-art amenities. The hotel's private beach access, expansive spa, and outdoor swimming pool offer a haven for relaxation. Dining options include gourmet restaurants that feature both international and local cuisine, with meals priced around €30 to €60 per person. For a truly luxurious experience, guests can book treatments at the Miramar Spa or enjoy personalized concierge services. For more information and reservations, visit their official website (https://www.granhotelmiramar.com).

Hotel Molina Lario: Located in the heart of Malaga's historic center, Hotel Molina Lario offers an intimate luxury experience with a contemporary touch. The hotel's rooftop terrace provides breathtaking views of the city and the Mediterranean, perfect for enjoying a cocktail or a meal from the on-site restaurant. Rooms feature modern decor with high-end amenities, and rates typically range from €150 to €300 per night. The hotel also boasts a well-equipped fitness center and a serene spa. Guests can savor fine dining at the hotel's restaurant, with prices averaging between €25 and €50 per meal. For bookings and further details, visit their official website (https://www.molinalario.com).

Villa Padierna Palace Hotel: Set against the backdrop of the Costa del Sol, Villa Padierna Palace Hotel exudes opulence. This five-star resort is renowned for its lush gardens, three golf courses, and a luxurious spa. Accommodations are designed with a classic Mediterranean flair, offering spacious rooms and suites. Prices for a night's stay start at approximately €200 and can go up significantly for premium suites. Dining is a high-end affair, with restaurants serving gourmet dishes at prices ranging from €40 to €80 per person. The hotel's exclusive services, including a private beach club and personalized butler service, make it a standout choice for an indulgent retreat. More information can be found on their official website (https://www.villapadierna.com).

Nobu Hotel Marbella: Just a short drive from Malaga, Nobu Hotel Marbella offers a blend of modern luxury and Japanese-inspired elegance. The hotel's sleek design is complemented by high-end amenities such as a world-class spa, a stylish rooftop bar, and an outdoor pool. Accommodations feature minimalist decor with luxurious touches, with rates starting from €250 per night. The on-site Nobu Restaurant serves renowned Japanese cuisine, with meal prices typically between €50 and €100. Guests can also enjoy exclusive access to the beach club and personalized concierge services. For reservations and more details, visit their official website (https://www.nobuhotels.com/marbella).

The Westin La Quinta Golf Resort & Spa: Located on the outskirts of Malaga, The Westin La Quinta Golf Resort & Spa is a sanctuary for golf enthusiasts and relaxation seekers. Set amidst sprawling gardens and lush fairways, the resort offers elegant rooms and suites with views of the golf course. Rates start at around €180 per night, with special packages available for extended stays. The resort features a full-service spa, multiple dining options with prices ranging from €30 to €70 per meal, and a well-regarded golf course. The Westin's tranquil setting and comprehensive facilities make it an ideal retreat for those looking to escape the bustle of city life. For more information and bookings, visit their official website (https://www.westinl quinta.com).

2.2 Budget-Friendly Options

Malaga also offers a range of budget-friendly accommodations that provide comfort and convenience without breaking the bank. These options are perfect for travelers seeking a value-for-money experience while exploring this enchanting city.

Hostal Sur Málaga: Hostal Sur Málaga is a charming budget option situated in the heart of Malaga. This family-run hostal offers cozy, clean rooms at affordable rates starting from €50 per night. The simple yet comfortable accommodations come with essential amenities like free Wi-Fi, air conditioning, and a daily breakfast service. Guests can enjoy a range of local dining options nearby, with meal prices typically around €10 to €20. The hostal's central location makes it easy to explore Malaga's main attractions on foot. For reservations and further details, visit their official website (https://www.hostalsurmálaga.com).

Hotel Sur Málaga: Another great budget choice, Hotel Sur Málaga, is conveniently located near the city center. The hotel provides basic yet comfortable rooms with amenities such as free Wi-Fi, a flat-screen TV, and a daily continental breakfast included in the room rate, which starts at approximately €60 per night. Guests can find various local eateries nearby, with average meal prices around €15 to €25. The hotel's proximity to public transportation and major attractions makes it a practical choice for budget-conscious travelers. More information and bookings can be found on their official website (https://www.hotelsurmálaga.com).

Ibis Málaga Centro Ciudad: For those seeking modern amenities at a reasonable price, Ibis Málaga Centro Ciudad is a standout option. Located in the city center, this hotel offers sleek rooms with contemporary decor starting at around €80 per night. Amenities include free Wi-Fi, a 24-hour snack bar, and a buffet breakfast with prices between €8 and €15. The hotel's central location provides easy access to Malaga's cultural landmarks and nightlife. For more details and to book a room, visit their official website (https://www.ibis.com/malaga-centro).

Málaga Premium Hotel: Situated near the city center, Málaga Premium Hotel offers a blend of comfort and affordability. Rooms are modern and well-equipped, with rates starting at approximately €70 per night. The hotel features complimentary Wi-Fi, a buffet breakfast service, and a lounge area. Nearby dining options offer budget-friendly meals averaging €10 to €20. The hotel's convenient location allows easy exploration of local attractions. For reservations and more information, visit their official website (https://www.malagapremiumhotel.com).

Casa de las Mercedes: Casa de las Mercedes is a charming guesthouse located in the historic center of Malaga. With rates starting at around €55 per night, it provides a cozy and affordable lodging option. The guesthouse features basic yet comfortable rooms, free Wi-Fi, and a shared kitchen for guests. The location is ideal for exploring nearby cafes and restaurants, with meal prices ranging from €10 to €20. For more details and bookings, visit their official website (https://www.casadelasmercedes.com).

2.3 Vacation Rentals and Apartments

Malaga offers a diverse selection of vacation rentals and apartments that provide a homey feel and flexibility for travelers seeking a more personalized experience. These options are ideal for families, groups, or anyone desiring a more independent stay while enjoying all the comforts of home.

Malaga Picasso Suites: Malaga Picasso Suites provides a stylish and comfortable home-away-from-home experience. Located in the city center, these modern apartments start at approximately €100 per night. Each suite is equipped with a full kitchen, living area, and free Wi-Fi, making it ideal for extended stays. The property is conveniently situated near local shops and restaurants, with meal costs ranging from €15 to €30. For more information and to book a stay, visit their official website (https://www.malagapicassosuites.com).

Apartamentos Soho Boutique: Offering a blend of contemporary design and practicality, Apartamentos Soho Boutique is located in the vibrant Soho district of Malaga. With rates starting at €90 per night, these well-appointed apartments include amenities such as a fully equipped kitchen, free Wi-Fi, and air conditioning. Guests can enjoy the lively neighborhood's dining and entertainment options, with average meal prices between €20 and €40. For reservations and further details, visit their official website (https://www.soho-boutique.com).

Ecoviajeros Hostel: Ecoviajeros Hostel offers eco-friendly vacation rental options with a focus on sustainability. Located in a central area of Malaga, the hostel features comfortable, eco-conscious accommodations starting at around €60 per night. Amenities include a shared kitchen, communal lounge, and free Wi-Fi. The hostel's location allows easy access to local eateries and attractions, with meal costs generally between €10 and €20. For more information and bookings, visit their official website (https://www.ecoviajeros.com).

La Casa del Poeta: La Casa del Poeta is a charming apartment located in Malaga's historic district. Offering a blend of traditional decor and modern amenities, the apartment starts at approximately €85 per night. It features a fully equipped kitchen, living space, and free Wi-Fi. The location is ideal for exploring nearby cafes and cultural sites, with average meal prices ranging from €15 to €30. For reservations and additional details, visit their official website (https://www.lacasadelpoeta.com).

Apartamento Plaza de la Merced: Situated in a prime location near Plaza de la Merced, this apartment offers a convenient and comfortable stay. With rates starting at €95 per night, the apartment includes amenities such as a full kitchen, living area, and complimentary Wi-Fi. Its central location makes it easy to explore local dining options, with average meal costs between €10 and €25. For more information and to book a stay, visit their official website (https://www.plazadelamerced.com).

2.4 Camping in Malaga
Camping in Malaga offers an excellent opportunity to immerse yourself in the natural beauty of the Costa del Sol while enjoying a range of modern amenities. The region's campgrounds cater to various preferences, from those seeking a basic outdoor experience to those desiring more luxurious amenities.

Camping La Bella Vista: Located on the outskirts of Malaga, Camping La Bella Vista is an idyllic retreat that provides stunning views of the surrounding landscape. Located in the town of Alhaurín de la Torre, this campsite features pitches for tents, caravans, and motorhomes. With prices starting at €25 per night, guests can enjoy spacious, shaded plots equipped with electricity. The site boasts a range of amenities including a swimming pool, restaurant, and grocery store. Unique features include organized activities for children and adults, as well as a local hiking trail that begins right at the campsite's edge. Meals at the on-site restaurant are reasonably priced, with a typical dinner costing around €15. For bookings and further details, visit their official website (http://www.campinglabellavista.com).

Camping Torremolinos: Located just a short drive from the vibrant city of Torremolinos, Camping Torremolinos offers an excellent blend of convenience and comfort. This family-friendly campsite is perfect for those who want to explore the city's beaches and nightlife while having a peaceful retreat to return to. Prices for accommodation start at €30 per night. The site features well-maintained pitches, a large swimming pool, and a children's playground. Notably, the campsite provides easy access to the beach and a range of on-site activities including a mini-golf course. Dining options include a restaurant and a snack bar, with average meal prices around €12. For more information and reservations, check their official website (http://www.campingtorrmolinos.com).

Camping El Pino: Situated in the heart of nature, Camping El Pino is located in the picturesque area of Mijas. This campsite offers a tranquil environment with pitches surrounded by pine trees. Prices begin at €22 per night, providing a budget-friendly option for travelers. Amenities include a swimming pool, a restaurant serving local cuisine, and sports facilities such as tennis courts. The site is known for its relaxed atmosphere and beautiful natural surroundings, making it ideal for nature enthusiasts. Meals at the restaurant cost approximately €10-15. For additional details and booking options, visit their official website (http://www.campingelpino.com).

Valle Niza Playa: For those seeking a coastal camping experience, Camping Valle Niza Playa provides direct access to the sandy shores of Valle-Niza beach. Located in the municipality of Vélez-Málaga, this campsite offers pitches with sea views starting at €28 per night. Guests can enjoy amenities such as a beach bar, a large swimming pool, and a range of water sports. Unique features include private beach access and evening entertainment. Meals at the on-site restaurant are around €18. For more information and to book your stay, visit their official website (http://www.campingvallenizaplaya.com).

Pueblo Blanco: Situated in the charming town of Mijas Pueblo, Camping Pueblo Blanco offers a blend of traditional Spanish ambiance and modern comforts. The campsite's prices start at €27 per night and include access to spacious pitches with electricity and water hookups. Amenities include a swimming pool, a restaurant with traditional Andalusian dishes, and organized activities. The campsite's proximity to Mijas Pueblo allows guests to explore the town's cultural heritage. Dining at the restaurant costs approximately €12. For more details and reservations, visit their official website (http://www.campingpuebloblanco.com).

2.5 Boutique Hotels

Boutique hotels in Malaga offer a unique and personalized experience, blending stylish accommodations with exceptional service. These charming establishments are perfect for travelers seeking a distinctive stay in one of Spain's most vibrant cities.

Hotel Molina Lario: Situated in the heart of Malaga's historic center, Hotel Molina Lario provides a luxurious retreat with a blend of modern elegance and traditional charm. Room rates start at approximately €150 per night, offering guests a range of well-appointed rooms and suites. The hotel features a rooftop terrace with stunning views of the cathedral, a fitness center, and a chic restaurant serving Mediterranean cuisine. Unique touches include personalized concierge services and an on-site art gallery showcasing local artists. Dining at the hotel's restaurant costs around €25-40 per meal. For more information and bookings, visit their official website (http://www.hotelmolinario.com).

Room Mate Valeria: Room Mate Valeria is a contemporary boutique hotel located near Malaga's port. Known for its stylish decor and vibrant atmosphere, this hotel offers rooms starting at €130 per night. Guests can enjoy amenities such as a rooftop pool, a trendy lounge bar, and a 24-hour front desk. The hotel's design is characterized by bold colors and modern art, creating a unique and lively environment. Breakfast is included in the room rate, and other meals at the hotel's restaurant are priced around €20-30. For further details and reservations, check their official website (http://www.room-matehotels.com/valeria).

Hotel Sur Málaga: Hotel Sur Málaga combines traditional Spanish hospitality with contemporary comforts. Located in the city's vibrant Soho district, room rates start at €110 per night. The hotel features cozy rooms, a communal lounge area, and a charming café that serves breakfast and light meals. Unique features include the hotel's focus on local culture, with art and décor reflecting Malaga's rich history. Meals at the café cost approximately €10-15. For more information and bookings, visit their official website (http://www.hotelsurmalaga.com).

Hotel Petit Palace Plaza Málaga: Hotel Petit Palace Plaza Málaga is a boutique gem in the city center, offering a blend of modern amenities and historic charm. Prices for rooms start at €120 per night. The hotel boasts features such as free Wi-Fi, a complimentary bicycle rental service, and a 24-hour business center. Guests can enjoy a rich breakfast buffet, with meals at the hotel's dining area priced around €15-20. Unique features include the hotel's eco-friendly practices and proximity to major attractions. For more information and to book, visit (http://www.petitpalaceplazamalaga.com).

2.6 Unique Stays: Historic Buildings and Beachfront Properties

Malaga offers a range of unique accommodations that provide memorable stays for discerning travelers. From historic buildings that whisper tales of the past to beachfront properties where the sea is just a step away, these exceptional lodgings combine distinctive charm with modern comforts. Each option presents its own unique features and services, ensuring that every stay in Malaga is as unique as the city itself.

Hotel La Bobadilla: Hotel La Bobadilla, a Royal Hideaway Hotel, is a luxurious gem located in the tranquil countryside near Loja. Set within a grand 19th-century palace, this unique property offers an opulent retreat amidst lush gardens and rolling hills. Room rates start at approximately €200 per night, reflecting the high standard of accommodation and service provided. Guests can enjoy spacious, elegantly decorated rooms with antique furnishings and modern amenities, including a full-service spa and an outdoor pool. The hotel's restaurant offers gourmet dining with a focus on local ingredients, with meal prices ranging from €50 to €70. Unique features of La Bobadilla include vineyard tours and wine-tasting experiences, which add a distinctive touch to the stay. For more information and reservations, visit their official website (http://www.barcelo.com/la-bobadilla).

Hotel La Viñuela & Spa: Hotel La Viñuela & Spa offers a unique experience set within a beautiful vineyard. This hotel is ideal for those who wish to combine relaxation with wine culture, as it offers exclusive access to the vineyard and its wine-tasting events. Room rates begin at €160 per night, providing guests with a luxurious stay in elegantly appointed rooms overlooking the vineyard. The property features a full-service spa, an outdoor pool, and fine dining at its restaurant, where meals are priced around €30 to €50. The hotel's unique vineyard tours and wine-pairing dinners are standout features, making it a perfect destination for wine lovers. For booking and further details, check their official website (http://www.lavinuelahotel.com).

Hotel El Castillo de Santa Catalina: Hotel El Castillo de Santa Catalina is a majestic accommodation perched on a hilltop, offering breathtaking views of Malaga and the surrounding coastline. Situated in a historic castle, this hotel combines medieval charm with modern luxury. With room rates starting at €180 per night, guests can enjoy rooms that blend traditional architecture with contemporary comfort. The castle features beautifully landscaped gardens, a swimming pool, and elegant dining options. Meals at the on-site restaurant cost between €40 and €60, reflecting the high quality of the cuisine. The castle's rich history and panoramic vistas make it a standout choice for a truly unique stay. For more information and reservations, visit their official website (http://www.castillodesantacatalina.com).

CHAPTER 3
TRANSPORTATION

3.1 Getting Around Malaga

Málaga offers a delightful blend of history, culture, and vibrant Mediterranean energy. Navigating this dynamic city effectively is key to fully immersing yourself in its offerings. Here are some essential tips to help you explore Málaga with ease and enjoy all that it has to offer.

Discover the Historic Center on Foot: The best way to experience the heart of Málaga is by walking through its historic center. Wander the charming streets of Plaza de la Merced and Calle Larios, where you'll find a mix of historic architecture, vibrant cafés, and local boutiques. Walking not only lets you appreciate the city's unique atmosphere but also allows you to stumble upon hidden treasures, such as quaint shops and delightful eateries, that you might miss when traveling by other means.

Make Use of the Local Bus System: Málaga's local bus network, operated by EMT (Empresa Malagueña de Transportes), is a practical way to cover longer distances and explore beyond the city center. The bus routes extend to major attractions like the Málaga Museum and the Port area. Buses run frequently throughout the day, and you can purchase tickets from vending machines or directly from the driver. Consider getting the "Tarjeta del Tercer Milenio" for unlimited travel within a specified period, which offers excellent value for tourists.

Rent a Bicycle or Scooter for Flexibility: For those who enjoy a bit of adventure, renting a bicycle or scooter provides a fun and flexible way to get around Málaga. With increasing bike lanes and paths, cycling is an enjoyable way to explore the city. Companies such as Málaga Bike and eScooter Málaga offer rentals throughout the city, allowing you to navigate along the scenic beach promenade or through picturesque parks. This mode of transport adds an extra layer of excitement to your visit and helps you cover more ground efficiently.

Utilize the Modern Metro System: Málaga's metro system, though relatively new, offers a quick and efficient way to traverse the city. The metro line connects key areas such as the city center, the university district, and the airport, making it a convenient option for travelers. Tickets are reasonably priced, and the system is user-friendly, with signs in both Spanish and English. The metro is a great choice for avoiding traffic and staying cool, especially during the warmer months.

Opt for a Taxi for Convenience: Taxis provide a comfortable and direct way to navigate Málaga, especially when traveling with luggage or in a group. Taxis are easily identifiable by their white color and are available at designated stands throughout the city or can be booked via phone or app. While slightly more expensive than public transport, taxis offer the advantage of direct routes and flexibility, making them a convenient choice for late-night travel or when heading to specific destinations.

3.2 Public Transportation Options

Málaga's public transportation network is designed to offer both convenience and accessibility to visitors and residents alike. The system includes buses, metro services, and commuter trains, each providing a reliable means to navigate the city and its surroundings.

Bus Services: The bus system in Málaga, managed by EMT (Empresa Malagueña de Transportes), forms the backbone of public transport within the city. With over 30 lines, the network covers a comprehensive range of destinations, from the central landmarks to outlying areas. Buses are frequent and operational from early morning until late evening. Tickets can be purchased directly from the driver or from vending machines located at various stops. The cost for a single ride is approximately €1.30. For tourists, the "Tarjeta del Tercer Milenio" offers unlimited travel for a designated period, providing excellent value for those planning to explore extensively.

Metro System: The Málaga Metro is a relatively recent addition to the city's transportation options, yet it offers a modern and efficient means of travel. The metro line connects major areas such as the city center, the university district, and the airport. With frequent services and comfortable trains, it provides a speedy alternative to road travel. Single journey tickets cost around €1.35, with options for multi-ride passes and travel cards for frequent use. The metro's simplicity and efficiency make it an excellent choice for navigating the city swiftly.

Commuter Trains: For those looking to explore beyond Málaga, the commuter train service operated by Renfe connects the city with neighboring towns and cities, such as Torremolinos and Fuengirola. The main train station, Málaga María Zambrano, is centrally located and well-connected to both the metro and bus systems. Train fares vary depending on the route, with prices starting at approximately €2.50 for shorter journeys. This service is a comfortable and scenic option for day trips and regional exploration.

Navigating Public Transport: To navigate Málaga's public transportation system effectively, consider using apps like "Malaga Bus" for real-time bus schedules and route information. For the metro, stations are well-marked in both Spanish and English, making it straightforward for visitors. The integration between different modes of transport ensures that transferring from buses to the metro is seamless.

Accessibility and Services: Málaga's public transportation system is generally accessible to people with disabilities. Buses feature low floors and designated spaces for wheelchairs, while metro stations are equipped with elevators and ramps. Additionally, information services and assistance are available to help visitors with special needs.

3.3 Car Rentals and Driving Tips

Renting a car in Málaga offers the freedom to explore the city and the beautiful Costa del Sol region at your own pace. With several reputable rental companies operating in the area, finding a car that suits your needs is straightforward. Here's a comprehensive guide to some of the best car rental options available in Málaga, including their locations, contact details, and pricing.

Enterprise Rent-A-Car: Located at Avenida de Velázquez, 109, Málaga, Enterprise Rent-A-Car offers a broad selection of vehicles ranging from compact cars to larger SUVs. The company is known for its excellent customer service and competitive rates. Daily rental prices start at approximately €25 for basic models. For reservations and further details, visit their website (https://www.enterprise.com).

Hertz: Hertz operates a convenient office at Málaga-Costa del Sol Airport, making it an ideal choice for travelers arriving by air. Hertz offers a diverse fleet and flexible rental options, with prices starting around €27 per day. Their website (https://www.hertz.com) provides detailed information on available vehicles and booking options.

Avis: Avis is situated at Calle Héroe de Sostoa, 9, Málaga. This company provides a wide range of vehicles and rental packages. Prices begin at approximately €30 per day. For booking and additional information, visit their website (https://www.avis.com).

Sixt: Sixt operates out of Avenida de la Palmera, 12, Málaga. Known for its affordable rental solutions, Sixt offers competitive rates starting from about €22 per day. For more details and reservations, check their website (https://www.sixt.com).

Goldcar: Goldcar is located at Calle Cruz del Humilladero, 118, Málaga. This company is recognized for its budget-friendly rental options, with prices starting around €20 per day. For reservations and further information, visit their website (https://www.goldcar.es).

Car Rental Prices and Booking Tips: Rental prices in Málaga can vary depending on the season, vehicle type, and rental duration. Generally, expect to pay between €20 to €30 per day for a standard car. Booking in advance can often secure better rates and ensure availability, especially during peak travel seasons.

Driving in Málaga: Driving in Málaga is relatively straightforward, with well-maintained roads and clear signage. The city's road network includes major routes like the A-7, which connects Málaga with other coastal towns. Parking in the city center can be challenging, so consider using public parking facilities or parking on the outskirts and using public transport to reach central areas.

3.4 Walking and Cycling in Malaga

Málaga, a sun-drenched gem on Spain's Costa del Sol, offers an inviting landscape for cycling and walking enthusiasts. With its mild climate, stunning coastal views, and historical charm, Málaga provides a rich tapestry of routes that cater to all levels of adventurers. From meandering through urban parks to tackling scenic coastal trails, the city ensures an enriching experience for every visitor.

Exploring Málaga by Bike

Cycling in Málaga is an exhilarating way to explore the city and its surroundings. The city's network of cycle paths and trails offers diverse experiences, from leisurely rides along the waterfront to more challenging routes through the hills.

Malaga Coastal Path: One notable route is the Malaga Coastal Path, which stretches from the city's port to the picturesque neighborhood of Pedregalejo. This flat, well-maintained path provides breathtaking views of the Mediterranean Sea and is ideal for both leisurely rides and family outings. The route is accessible for all skill levels, and bike rentals are available at various locations along the route. Prices for bike rentals typically range from €15 to €25 per day, depending on the bike type and rental duration.

Gibralfaro Hill Circuit: For those seeking a more rugged experience, the Gibralfaro Hill Circuit offers a challenging ride with rewarding panoramic views of the city. This route takes cyclists up the steep slopes of Gibralfaro Hill, where the ancient castle stands. The climb is demanding, but the vistas from the top are worth the effort. It's advisable to rent a mountain bike for this route, with rental prices around €20 to €30 per day. Local bike shops provide detailed maps and guidance on navigating the more difficult sections.

Málaga to Torremolinos Coastal Route: The Málaga to Torremolinos Coastal Route is perfect for those looking to combine cycling with a beach outing. This longer route covers approximately 20 kilometers and runs along the coastline, connecting Málaga with the neighboring city of Torremolinos. The path is mostly flat and offers a refreshing sea breeze, making it a pleasant ride. This route is well-suited for road bikes, and rentals are available at around €25 to €35 per day.

Parque de Málaga: Cyclists interested in a more relaxed ride can explore the Parque de Málaga area. This park features several dedicated bike paths and is ideal for casual rides amidst lush greenery and historical monuments. It's a great spot for families and beginners, with bike rentals typically costing between €15 and €20 per day.

Sierra de las Nieves National Park: For those who want to explore beyond the city limits, the Sierra de las Nieves National Park provides a spectacular mountain biking experience. This route requires a bit more preparation and a sturdy mountain bike, with rentals priced around €30 to €50 per day. The park offers a range of trails suitable for various skill levels, with options for guided tours available.

Walking Through Málaga: Walking through Málaga allows visitors to immerse themselves in the city's rich history and vibrant culture. The city boasts a variety of pedestrian-friendly routes, each offering unique insights into Málaga's heritage and natural beauty.

Paseo del Parque: A leisurely stroll along the Paseo del Parque is a must for anyone exploring Málaga on foot. This beautiful promenade, lined with exotic plants and sculptures, provides a serene environment for walkers. It's an excellent spot to appreciate Málaga's botanical diversity and historical landmarks, including the impressive City Hall.

Historic Center Walk: The Historic Center Walk is perfect for those interested in Málaga's architectural and cultural heritage. This route takes visitors through the city's charming old town, showcasing landmarks such as the Málaga Cathedral, the Roman Theatre, and the Alcazaba. Walking this route allows travelers to appreciate the city's blend of historical and modern influences, with plenty of opportunities for shopping and dining along the way.

Montes de Málaga Natural Park: For a more nature-focused experience, the Montes de Málaga Natural Park offers a network of trails through lush forested areas and rugged terrain. These trails cater to various fitness levels and provide stunning views of the surrounding landscape. It's advisable to wear comfortable hiking shoes and bring sufficient water, as some trails can be quite demanding.

Malagueta Beach Promenade: The Malagueta Beach Promenade is ideal for those who want to combine a beach day with a leisurely walk. This route runs along the sandy shores of Malagueta Beach, offering stunning sea views and a refreshing sea breeze. It's a great spot for a relaxing walk, with plenty of cafes and restaurants to stop for a drink or a meal.

Caminito del Rey: Finally, the Caminito del Rey, located a short drive from Málaga, is renowned for its dramatic cliffside walkways and breathtaking views. This route requires advance booking and is best suited for those seeking a more adventurous hiking experience. Safety equipment is provided, and guided tours are available for a more comprehensive experience.

3.5 Boat Tours and Water Sports

Málaga, with its stunning Mediterranean coastline and inviting azure waters, is a haven for those eager to explore the sea. From thrilling water sports to serene boat tours, the city offers a diverse range of maritime activities that cater to all tastes. Whether you're seeking an adrenaline rush or a peaceful sail along the coast, Málaga's boat tours and water sports have something for everyone.

Discovering Boat Tours

Embarking on a boat tour in Málaga provides a unique perspective of the city's stunning coastline and landmarks. The following companies offer a variety of tours, each showcasing the beauty of Málaga's waters in different ways.

Málaga Boat Tours: Málaga Boat Tours offers a range of options for those interested in exploring the city's maritime surroundings. Located at the Port of Málaga, this company provides both private and group tours, including sunset cruises and dolphin-watching excursions. Their boats are well-equipped for comfort, and the guides are knowledgeable about local marine life and history. Prices for a 2-hour tour typically range from €30 to €50 per person. For more details or to make a reservation, visit their website at (http://malagaboattours.com).

Costa del Sol Cruises: Costa del Sol Cruises offers luxurious sailing experiences along the coast of Málaga. Their services include private yacht charters and themed cruises, such as wine tasting or tapas tours on the water. Based at the Real Club Mediterráneo de Málaga, Costa del Sol Cruises caters to both small and large groups, providing a high-end experience with impeccable service. Prices vary significantly depending on the type of cruise and duration, starting from around €250 for a private yacht rental. For more information, visit (http://costadelsolcruises.com).

Ocean Adventure Málaga: Ocean Adventure Málaga specializes in family-friendly boat tours, including pirate-themed cruises and snorkeling excursions. Located at the Marina Málaga, their tours are designed to be entertaining and educational for children and adults alike. Prices for their family tours start at approximately €25 per person. To book a tour or for more details, check their website at (http://oceanadventuremalaga.com).

Mediterranean Sailing: Mediterranean Sailing provides a range of sailing experiences from leisurely day trips to full-week charters. Their services include guided tours of the Málaga Bay area and the nearby Marbella coastline. Based at the Puerto de Benalmádena, their luxurious sailboats are ideal for those looking to explore the region's beautiful coastline in style. Prices start at around €200 for a day trip, with extended charters available upon request. Visit their website at (http://mediterraneansailing.com) for more information.

Aqua Adventure: Aqua Adventure offers exciting speedboat and jet ski rentals for those who prefer a more exhilarating maritime experience. Located near Playa de la Malagueta, Aqua Adventure provides a range of high-speed options for thrill-seekers. Their fleet includes modern jet skis and powerful speedboats, with prices starting at approximately €60 per hour for jet skis and €150 for a half-day speedboat rental. For details and bookings, visit (http://aquadventuremalaga.com).

Engaging in Water Sports

Málaga's warm waters and favorable winds make it an ideal destination for a wide array of water sports. From surfing to paddleboarding, the city offers activities that cater to both beginners and seasoned enthusiasts.

Surf School Málaga: Surf School Málaga provides lessons and equipment rentals for surfers of all levels. Located at Playa de la Victoria, this school offers surfboards and wetsuits for rent, with lessons tailored to various skill levels. Prices for surf lessons start around €40 per person for a 2-hour session, including equipment. For more details, check their website at (http://surfschoolmalaga.com).

Paddle Surf Málaga: Paddle Surf Málaga specializes in stand-up paddleboarding (SUP) experiences. Their services include rentals and guided tours along Málaga's scenic coastline. Located at Playa de la Malagueta, Paddle Surf Málaga offers SUP boards and paddles, with rental prices starting at approximately €25 per hour. Guided tours are available for those looking to explore the local marine environment. Visit (http://paddlesurfmalaga.com) for more information.

Kitesurfing Málaga: Kitesurfing Málaga caters to kitesurfing enthusiasts, offering lessons and equipment rentals for all levels. Based at Playa de los Álamos, this company provides comprehensive kitesurfing courses and equipment, with prices starting at €70 for a 2-hour lesson. For more details, check their website at (http://kitesurfingmalaga.com).

Scuba Diving Málaga: Scuba Diving Málaga offers a range of diving experiences, from beginner courses to advanced dives. Located at the Port of Málaga, their services include guided dives and equipment rentals. Prices for a single dive start at around €50, with discounts available for multiple dives or courses. Visit (http://scubadivingmalaga.com) for more information and bookings.

Jet Ski Málaga: Jet Ski Málaga provides high-octane jet ski rentals for those seeking an adrenaline rush. Situated at the Marina Málaga, their fleet includes the latest models for a thrilling ride on the water. Rental prices start at €70 per hour. For more details, visit (http://jetskimalaga.com).

CHAPTER 4
TOP 10 ATTRACTIONS & HIDDEN GEMS

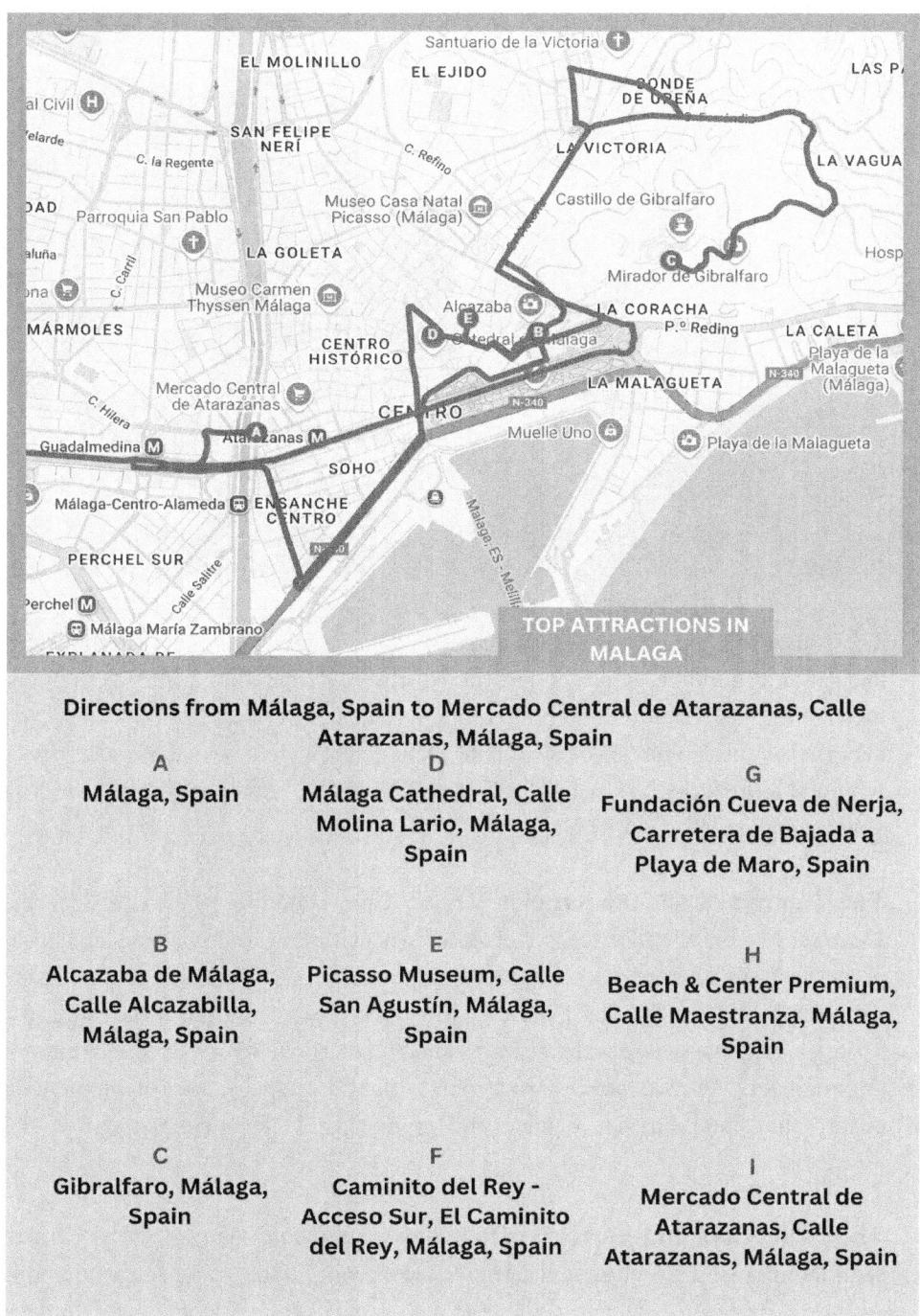

Directions from Málaga, Spain to Mercado Central de Atarazanas, Calle Atarazanas, Málaga, Spain

A
Málaga, Spain

B
Alcazaba de Málaga, Calle Alcazabilla, Málaga, Spain

C
Gibralfaro, Málaga, Spain

D
Málaga Cathedral, Calle Molina Lario, Málaga, Spain

E
Picasso Museum, Calle San Agustín, Málaga, Spain

F
Caminito del Rey - Acceso Sur, El Caminito del Rey, Málaga, Spain

G
Fundación Cueva de Nerja, Carretera de Bajada a Playa de Maro, Spain

H
Beach & Center Premium, Calle Maestranza, Málaga, Spain

I
Mercado Central de Atarazanas, Calle Atarazanas, Málaga, Spain

4.1 Alcazaba Fortress

The Alcazaba Fortress in Málaga stands as a testament to the city's rich history and cultural heritage. This monumental fortress, perched on a hill overlooking the vibrant city below, offers visitors a chance to step back in time and experience the grandeur of Moorish architecture. Here are must-visit spots within this historical gem that will captivate your imagination and leave you yearning for more.

The Courtyard of the Orange Trees: Upon entering the Alcazaba, the Courtyard of the Orange Trees welcomes you with its serene beauty. This lush, green oasis is adorned with fragrant orange trees, providing a peaceful escape from the hustle and bustle of the city. The courtyard's design reflects traditional Moorish gardens, where water features and symmetrical layouts create a tranquil environment. As you stroll through this charming space, take a moment to absorb the historical significance and architectural elegance that define the Alcazaba.

The Main Gate and Torre del Homenaje: The Main Gate of the Alcazaba, with its imposing structure and intricate stonework, is the grand entrance to this historical fortress. Adjacent to the gate stands the Torre del Homenaje (Homage

Tower), a formidable defensive structure that once served as the main keep. Climb to the top of the tower and be rewarded with panoramic views of Málaga and the surrounding coastline. The imposing architecture and strategic location of this tower offer a glimpse into the fortress's military past.

The Archaeological Museum: Situated within the Alcazaba's walls is the Archaeological Museum, which houses a fascinating collection of artifacts from Málaga's past. Here, you can explore ancient Roman, Moorish, and pre-Moorish relics that provide insight into the region's diverse history. The museum's exhibits are thoughtfully curated to highlight the significance of each artifact, making it an educational and enriching experience.

The Alcazaba's Walkways: The Alcazaba's labyrinthine walkways and narrow passages are a delight for explorers. As you wander through these historic paths, you'll encounter hidden corners, scenic viewpoints, and remnants of ancient defensive structures. The walkways not only offer a glimpse into the fortress's defensive mechanisms but also provide stunning views of the city and the Mediterranean Sea.

The Gardens and Water Features: Scattered throughout the Alcazaba are beautifully designed gardens and water features that enhance the fortress's charm. The lush vegetation, along with the soothing sound of flowing water, creates a serene atmosphere. These gardens are not just aesthetically pleasing but also serve as a reminder of the Moorish emphasis on harmony between architecture and nature.

4.2 Gibralfaro Castle

Gibralfaro Castle is a must-see for anyone interested in history, architecture, and stunning views. Its strategic position and historical significance make it a fascinating destination that captures the essence of Málaga's rich heritage.

The Majestic Heights of Gibralfaro Castle: Perched atop a hill, Gibralfaro Castle offers an awe-inspiring view of Málaga and the surrounding landscape. This historic fortress, dating back to the 14th century, is not only a symbol of the city's medieval past but also a vantage point that allows visitors to experience the beauty of Málaga from above. Here are five compelling reasons to visit Gibralfaro Castle and soak in its historical and scenic splendor.

Panoramic Views from the Ramparts: One of the main attractions of Gibralfaro Castle is its breathtaking panoramic views. As you walk along the ramparts, you'll be treated to a stunning vista of Málaga's skyline, the Mediterranean Sea, and the surrounding mountains. The elevated perspective provides an excellent opportunity for photography and allows you to appreciate the strategic importance of the castle's location.

The Castle's Historical Significance: Gibralfaro Castle holds a significant place in Málaga's history. Originally built by the Nasrid dynasty in the 14th century, the castle was designed as a defensive stronghold. Its historical relevance is evident in the well-preserved defensive walls and towers. Exploring these features provides insight into the military strategies and architectural innovations of the time.

The Fortress Walls and Towers: The castle's fortress walls and towers are a testament to its formidable design. Strolling along these ancient walls gives you a sense of the strength and durability of the structure. The towers, including the Torre de las Armas and Torre de la Vela, offer unique perspectives and insights into the defensive mechanisms employed during the castle's operational days.

The Museum of the History of the Castle: Within the castle grounds, you'll find the Museum of the History of the Castle, which offers an informative look into the fortress's past. The museum's exhibits include historical documents, models of the castle, and artifacts that reveal the evolution of Gibralfaro Castle from its origins to the present day.

The Beautiful Gardens: The gardens surrounding Gibralfaro Castle are a serene escape from the historical exploration. The well-maintained gardens offer a pleasant place to relax and take in the views. With lush vegetation and scenic spots, the gardens enhance the overall experience and provide a perfect setting for a leisurely stroll.

4.3 Malaga Cathedral

Málaga Cathedral, often referred to as "La Manquita" (the One-Armed Lady) due to its unfinished south tower, is a marvel of architectural splendor. This Renaissance masterpiece, located in the heart of Málaga, showcases intricate design and historical significance. Here are remarkable aspects of the Málaga Cathedral that will make your visit unforgettable.

The Grand Facade: The grand facade of Málaga Cathedral is a striking example of Renaissance architecture. The intricately carved stonework, featuring ornate details and majestic columns, creates an impressive entrance to the cathedral. As you approach the facade, you'll be captivated by its grandeur and the artistic craftsmanship that defines this architectural gem.

The Interior's Rich Decor: Stepping inside Málaga Cathedral, you are greeted by a lavishly decorated interior that exudes elegance. The high, vaulted ceilings, intricate woodwork, and stunning stained glass windows create a serene and awe-inspiring atmosphere. The cathedral's interior is a feast for the eyes, with every detail meticulously crafted to reflect its religious and cultural significance.

The Choir Stalls: One of the cathedral's highlights is the beautifully carved choir stalls. These intricately designed wooden seats, adorned with detailed sculptures and decorative elements, showcase the artistry of the Renaissance period. The choir stalls are not only functional but also serve as a testament to the cathedral's artistic and architectural heritage.

The Cathedral Museum: The Cathedral Museum, located within the cathedral complex, offers a fascinating glimpse into the history and art of Málaga Cathedral. The museum's collection includes religious artifacts, historical documents, and artworks that provide context and background to the cathedral's development and significance.

The Views from the Tower: Although the south tower remains unfinished, it offers a unique vantage point for visitors. Climbing the tower provides panoramic views of Málaga and its surrounding landscape. The partially completed tower adds a touch of intrigue and historical context to your visit, highlighting the cathedral's evolving story.

4.4 Picasso Museum

The Picasso Museum in Málaga is a tribute to one of the 20th century's most influential artists, Pablo Picasso. Located in the heart of the city where Picasso was born, the museum offers an intimate look into the life and work of this artistic genius. Here are compelling reasons to visit the Picasso Museum and immerse yourself in its creative legacy.

A Collection of Masterpieces: The Picasso Museum boasts an impressive collection of over 200 works by Pablo Picasso, spanning his entire career. From early sketches to later masterpieces, the museum's collection offers a comprehensive overview of Picasso's artistic evolution. Each piece provides insight into his innovative techniques and creative vision.

The Museum's Historic Setting: The museum is housed in the Palacio de Buenavista, a stunning 16th-century mansion that enhances the experience with its historical charm. The palace's architecture, combined with the museum's art collection, creates a captivating environment that beautifully contrasts with and complements Picasso's modern works.

Temporary Exhibitions: In addition to its permanent collection, the Picasso Museum regularly hosts temporary exhibitions that explore various aspects of Picasso's life and work. These exhibitions often feature rare and unique pieces, offering fresh perspectives and deepening your understanding of the artist's multifaceted career.

Educational Programs and Workshops: The museum offers a range of educational programs and workshops designed to engage visitors of all ages. These programs include guided tours, art workshops, and lectures that delve into Picasso's techniques and artistic contributions. Participating in these activities provides a more interactive and immersive experience.

The Museum Café: The museum's café is a delightful spot to relax and reflect on your visit. With its charming ambiance and views of the surrounding architecture, the café provides a perfect setting to enjoy a coffee or light snack. It's an excellent place to unwind after exploring the museum's exhibits.

4.5 Caminito del Rey

Caminito del Rey, often dubbed the "King's Little Pathway," is a spectacular walkway that offers a thrilling adventure through some of Spain's most dramatic landscapes. This historic path, set high above a gorge, promises an exhilarating experience for those seeking both beauty and excitement. Here are unforgettable aspects of Caminito del Rey that will make your visit truly memorable.

The Dramatic Cliffside Path: The Caminito del Rey is renowned for its narrow, cliffside walkway that clings to the edge of a deep gorge. As you traverse the path, suspended high above the ground, you'll be treated to breathtaking views of the surrounding natural beauty. The sheer drop and stunning vistas create a sense of awe and adventure that is both exhilarating and humbling.

The Historical Significance: Originally built in the early 20th century for workers accessing a hydroelectric plant, Caminito del Rey has a rich historical background. The path's restoration in recent years has preserved its historical essence while making it accessible to modern adventurers. Learning about the path's history adds depth to the experience and highlights its engineering marvel.

The Spectacular Scenery: The journey along Caminito del Rey is a visual feast, with stunning scenery that includes rugged cliffs, lush vegetation, and crystal-clear waters. The contrast between the rugged terrain and the vibrant natural surroundings creates a dramatic and picturesque backdrop that enhances the overall experience.

The Thrill of the Suspended Walkways: One of the most exhilarating aspects of Caminito del Rey is the series of suspended walkways and bridges that extend across the gorge. These walkways provide a unique and thrilling perspective of the landscape, offering a sense of adventure as you navigate the high-altitude pathways.

The Adventure and Safety Measures: While Caminito del Rey offers an adrenaline-pumping adventure, safety is a top priority. The path is equipped with safety rails and guided tours to ensure a secure experience for all visitors. The combination of excitement and safety measures makes it an accessible adventure for those seeking a memorable and safe outdoor experience.

4.6 Nerja Caves

Perched on the sun-drenched coast of Málaga, Spain, the Nerja Caves (Cueva de Nerja) are a breathtaking natural wonder that beckon travelers from around the globe. This subterranean marvel, with its intricate labyrinth of caverns and stunning formations, promises an experience unlike any other. Here's a detailed look at five must-see highlights within these ancient caves, each offering a unique glimpse into the mysterious world beneath the surface.

The Great Hall (Sala de la Gran Cueva): As you descend into the Nerja Caves, the Great Hall immediately captures your imagination with its vast, cathedral-like space. Spanning over 100 meters in length and 50 meters in height, this chamber is one of the largest in Europe. The sheer scale of the hall, coupled with its majestic stalactites and stalagmites, creates an awe-inspiring atmosphere that feels almost otherworldly. Standing in this colossal space, you can't help but feel a profound sense of wonder at the natural forces that shaped it over millennia.

The Prehistoric Cave Paintings: Among the most captivating features of the Nerja Caves are the prehistoric cave paintings discovered in the cave's depths. These ancient artworks, estimated to be around 20,000 years old, provide a fascinating glimpse into the lives of our distant ancestors. The paintings, which include depictions of animals and abstract symbols, are a testament to the artistic expression of early humans. The sight of these primitive masterpieces, illuminated by subtle lighting, evokes a deep connection to the past and the people who once roamed these very caves.

The Christmas Tree Stalactite (La Estalactita de Navidad): One of the most enchanting formations within the Nerja Caves is the Christmas Tree Stalactite. Named for its resemblance to a decorated holiday tree, this stunning formation is a testament to the natural artistry found within the cave system. The delicate, branching stalactite, adorned with glistening mineral deposits, captures the imagination and adds a whimsical touch to the cave's underground landscape. Its beauty is accentuated by the carefully designed lighting, which highlights the intricate details of this natural wonder.

The Bell Chamber (Sala de la Campana): The Bell Chamber, so named for its acoustics that resemble the sound of bells, offers a unique auditory experience in addition to its visual splendor. As you enter this chamber, you'll notice how the natural echoes create a symphony of sounds that enhance the ambiance of the space. The chamber is adorned with a variety of formations, including delicate draperies and towering columns, each adding to the room's ethereal quality. The combination of sight and sound in the Bell Chamber creates a truly immersive experience.

The Lost River (Río Perdido): In the depths of the Nerja Caves, you'll discover the Lost River, an underground stream that adds a dynamic element to the cave's landscape. The river, with its crystal-clear waters and gently flowing current, provides a serene contrast to the rocky formations that surround it. As you follow the river's course, you'll encounter picturesque pools and cascading waterfalls, each offering a glimpse into the cave's vibrant ecosystem. The tranquil beauty of the Lost River makes it a memorable part of your subterranean adventure.

4.7 La Malagueta Beach

La Malagueta Beach, located in the heart of Málaga, is a vibrant and inviting destination that perfectly captures the essence of the Spanish Mediterranean coast. With its golden sands, crystal-clear waters, and lively atmosphere, this beach offers an array of experiences that promise to delight every visitor. Here's a closer look at must-see spots and activities at La Malagueta Beach that will make your visit to Málaga truly unforgettable.

The Beachfront Promenade (Paseo Marítimo): Strolling along the Paseo Marítimo, the beachfront promenade that stretches alongside La Malagueta Beach, is a quintessential Málaga experience. This lively walkway is lined with palm trees, charming cafes, and vibrant shops, making it the perfect place for a leisurely afternoon stroll. As you walk, you'll enjoy breathtaking views of the Mediterranean Sea and the city's skyline. The promenade's lively atmosphere, combined with its stunning scenery, creates a delightful setting for relaxation and people-watching.

The Beachfront Chiringuitos (Beach Bars): No visit to La Malagueta Beach is complete without experiencing the local flavor at one of the beachfront chiringuitos. These casual beach bars offer a taste of traditional Spanish cuisine, with dishes such as fried fish (pescaito frito) and refreshing gazpacho. The laid-back ambiance of the chiringuitos, coupled with their prime location right on the sand, makes them the perfect spot to enjoy a meal while taking in the sea breeze and beautiful views.

The Mediterranean Sunsets: One of the most enchanting aspects of La Malagueta Beach is its breathtaking sunsets. As the day draws to a close, the sky transforms into a canvas of vibrant colors, with hues of pink, orange, and purple reflecting off the tranquil waters. Finding a comfortable spot on the beach or along the promenade to watch the sunset is a must-do experience. The sheer beauty of the Mediterranean sunset creates a magical moment that is sure to leave a lasting impression.

The Beachfront Sports Activities: For those who enjoy staying active, La Malagueta Beach offers a range of sports activities to suit all interests. From beach volleyball and paddleboarding to windsurfing and beach soccer, there's something for everyone. The beach's ample space and favorable weather conditions make it an ideal location for both casual and competitive sports. Joining in on the fun or simply watching others play adds an exciting dynamic to your beach day.

The Nearby Parque de Malaga: Adjacent to La Malagueta Beach, the Parque de Malaga provides a lush green escape from the sun and sand. This beautifully landscaped park features shaded paths, colorful flowerbeds, and tranquil fountains. It's the perfect spot for a leisurely walk or a relaxing picnic. The park's proximity to the beach allows you to easily transition from sunbathing to enjoying a serene natural setting.

4.8 Mercado de Atarazanas

Mercado de Atarazanas, Málaga's historic market, is a bustling hub of activity and a vibrant showcase of local culture and cuisine. Situated in the heart of the city, this market offers an immersive experience that celebrates the rich flavors and traditions of Andalusia. Here's a closer look at key highlights of Mercado de Atarazanas that will make your visit to Málaga a memorable culinary adventure.

The Market Architecture: As you approach Mercado de Atarazanas, you'll be struck by its striking architecture. The market is housed in a 14th-century Moorish building, which was originally a shipyard. The beautifully restored façade, with its intricate Moorish arches and colorful tiles, sets the stage for the vibrant market experience that awaits inside. The blend of historic and modern elements creates a unique and inviting atmosphere that enhances your visit.

The Fresh Produce Stalls: The heart of Mercado de Atarazanas is its bustling fresh produce stalls, where you'll find an array of vibrant fruits and vegetables. The market's vendors take pride in offering locally grown produce, from juicy oranges and sweet strawberries to crisp lettuce and fragrant herbs. The sheer variety and freshness of the produce are a testament to the region's agricultural bounty. Sampling some of the local fruits or picking up ingredients for a picnic is a delightful way to experience the market's offerings.

The Artisanal Cheese and Charcuterie: For cheese and charcuterie enthusiasts, Mercado de Atarazanas is a treasure trove of delicious finds. The market features an array of artisanal cheeses, from creamy Manchego to tangy Cabrales, as well as a selection of cured meats such as jamón ibérico and chorizo. The knowledgeable vendors are always happy to offer samples and recommendations, allowing you to explore the rich flavors of Spanish cheeses and cured meats. The experience of tasting these local delicacies is a highlight of any visit to the market.

The Seafood Delights: Málaga is renowned for its seafood, and Mercado de Atarazanas is the place to experience it firsthand. The market's seafood stalls offer a dazzling array of fresh catches, including succulent prawns, tender octopus, and locally caught fish. The display of glistening seafood is both impressive and inviting. Whether you're looking to cook a seafood feast at home or simply sample some fresh seafood on the go, the market's offerings are sure to delight your taste buds.

The Traditional Tapas and Local Delicacies: In addition to its fresh produce and artisanal products, Mercado de Atarazanas is home to several stalls offering traditional Spanish tapas and local delicacies. From savory croquettes and flavorful empanadas to sweet pastries and olives, the market provides a taste of Andalusian cuisine. Enjoying these tapas while soaking in the lively atmosphere of the market is a delightful way to experience the local food culture.

4.9 El Palo Neighborhood

El Palo, a charming neighborhood in Málaga, offers a delightful blend of traditional Spanish charm and coastal allure. Known for its relaxed atmosphere and local character, El Palo is a hidden gem that invites visitors to explore its unique attractions and vibrant community. Here's a detailed look at must-visit spots in El Palo that will give you a true sense of this endearing Málaga neighborhood.

The El Palo Beach: The centerpiece of the El Palo neighborhood is its picturesque beach, which offers a more laid-back alternative to the bustling city beaches. With its golden sands and clear waters, El Palo Beach is a perfect spot for sunbathing, swimming, and enjoying the Mediterranean climate. The beach's relaxed vibe and scenic views make it an ideal place to unwind and soak up the local atmosphere.

The Fishermen's Neighborhood (Barrio de los Pescadores): El Palo's Fishermen's Neighborhood, or Barrio de los Pescadores, is a vibrant area that showcases the district's maritime heritage. The narrow, winding streets are lined with traditional fisherman's houses, and the local fishing boats can often be seen docked along the shore. This area provides a glimpse into the daily life of El Palo's fishing community and offers a unique perspective on the neighborhood's cultural history.

The El Palo Promenade (Paseo Marítimo El Palo): For a leisurely stroll with stunning views, the El Palo Promenade is a must-visit. This scenic walkway stretches along the coast, offering picturesque vistas of the Mediterranean Sea and the surrounding coastline. The promenade is lined with charming cafes and restaurants where you can enjoy a meal or a drink while taking in the beautiful sea views. It's the perfect place to relax and savor the laid-back atmosphere of El Palo.

The Local Tapas Bars: El Palo is home to a number of local tapas bars that offer a taste of authentic Andalusian cuisine. These cozy establishments serve up a variety of traditional dishes, from delicious fried fish to savory montaditos (small sandwiches). The warm and welcoming ambiance of the tapas bars, combined with the flavorful local dishes, creates a delightful dining experience that captures the essence of El Palo's culinary scene.

The El Palo Market: The El Palo Market, or Mercado de El Palo, is a lively spot where locals shop for fresh produce, seafood, and other goods. The market's vibrant atmosphere and diverse offerings provide a glimpse into the daily life of the neighborhood. Whether you're looking to pick up some fresh ingredients or simply explore the local vendors, the El Palo Market is a great place to experience the community's authentic flavor.

4.10 Mijas Pueblo

Perched on a hill overlooking the Costa del Sol, Mijas Pueblo is a charming white-washed village that offers a picturesque escape from the bustling city life. Known for its traditional Andalusian architecture, stunning views, and warm hospitality, Mijas Pueblo is a must-visit destination in Málaga. Here's a detailed look at captivating spots in Mijas Pueblo that will make your visit truly enchanting.

The Mijas Pueblo Town Square (Plaza de las Flores): At the heart of Mijas Pueblo lies the Plaza de las Flores, a vibrant town square that embodies the essence of Andalusian charm. Surrounded by colorful flowerbeds and traditional buildings, the square is a delightful place to relax and soak in the local atmosphere. The plaza is also home to a number of cafes and shops where you can enjoy a coffee or browse for souvenirs. The inviting ambiance and picturesque surroundings make the Plaza de las Flores a perfect starting point for your exploration of Mijas Pueblo.

The Mijas Bullring (Plaza de Toros): The Mijas Bullring, or Plaza de Toros, is a fascinating historical site that offers insight into Spain's bullfighting tradition. This charming, circular arena is one of the oldest in the region and provides a glimpse into the cultural heritage of Andalusia. The bullring's classic design and serene setting, surrounded by lush greenery, make it an intriguing spot to visit. Guided tours are available, offering a deeper understanding of the bullring's history and significance.

The Mijas Donkey Taxis: A unique and endearing feature of Mijas Pueblo is its donkey taxis, a traditional mode of transportation that adds a touch of whimsy to your visit. These charming donkey-drawn carts offer a leisurely way to explore the village's narrow streets and picturesque corners. The friendly donkeys and their attentive handlers provide a fun and memorable experience for visitors of all ages. Riding in a donkey taxi is a delightful way to experience the village's charm and history.

The Mijas Artisan Workshops: Mijas Pueblo is known for its vibrant artisan community, and a visit to the local workshops offers a chance to see traditional crafts in action. From pottery and ceramics to handcrafted jewelry and textiles, the artisan workshops showcase the talents of local craftsmen and women. Many workshops offer demonstrations and the opportunity to purchase unique, handmade items. Exploring these workshops provides a deeper appreciation for the village's rich artistic heritage.

The Mijas Pueblo Viewpoints: The scenic viewpoints in Mijas Pueblo offer some of the most breathtaking vistas on the Costa del Sol. From various vantage points around the village, you can enjoy panoramic views of the Mediterranean Sea, the surrounding countryside, and the distant mountains. These viewpoints are perfect for capturing memorable photographs or simply taking a moment to admire the stunning natural beauty of the area.

4.11 Outdoor Activities and Adventures

Málaga, with its stunning coastal setting and diverse landscapes, offers a rich array of sports, outdoor activities, and adventures that cater to every kind of enthusiast. From exhilarating water sports to scenic hikes, the city is a playground for those seeking both relaxation and excitement. Below are exceptional activities that showcase Málaga's vibrant outdoor culture.

Exploring the Mediterranean: The Costa del Sol, stretching along Málaga's coastline, is a haven for water sports enthusiasts. The warm Mediterranean waters provide the perfect backdrop for activities such as windsurfing, kitesurfing, and stand-up paddleboarding. Locations like Playa de la Malagueta and Playa de la Caleta are particularly popular for these sports. The calm and inviting waters make these activities accessible for beginners, while the more challenging waves cater to experienced practitioners. Prices for water sports lessons generally range from €50 to €80 for a two-hour session, depending on the activity and equipment provided. For those interested in diving, the nearby waters around the Maro-Cerro Gordo Cliffs Natural Area offer spectacular underwater experiences. Companies such as "Malaga Diving" provide guided diving tours and equipment rental. Visit their official website for more details and bookings: (https://www.malagadiving.com).

Mountain Adventures: The Montes de Málaga, a mountain range just north of the city, is a prime destination for hiking and rock climbing. This natural park boasts a network of trails that offer a range of difficulty levels, from easy walks to challenging hikes. The trails meander through dense forests, offering glimpses of local wildlife and panoramic views of the city and coast. For rock climbing enthusiasts, the area around El Chorro Gorge presents numerous climbing routes, catering to various skill levels. Guided hikes and climbing sessions are available, with prices typically starting from €40 for a half-day excursion. To explore these adventures further, check out "Andalucía Adventure," which provides comprehensive information and bookings on their website: (https://www.andalucia-adventure.com).

Thrilling Heights: For a bird's-eye view of Málaga, paragliding offers an unmatched perspective. Launch sites around the city, such as those near Mijas or Benalmádena, provide the perfect conditions for this exhilarating activity. Soaring above the Costa del Sol, participants can enjoy breathtaking vistas of the Mediterranean Sea, rolling hills, and picturesque towns. Tandem paragliding experiences, suitable for beginners, generally cost between €120 and €180 for a 20 to 30-minute flight. These flights include all necessary equipment and a professional instructor. To book an unforgettable paragliding experience, visit "Skydive Spain" at (https://www.skydive-spain.com).

Adventure in the Caves: The Cueva del Tesoro, or Treasure Cave, located in Rincón de la Victoria, is one of the few marine caves in Spain. Guided tours of the cave reveal stunning underground formations and fascinating geological features. The cave is renowned for its unique stalactite and stalagmite formations, which create an otherworldly experience. Tours are typically priced around €10 to €15 per person and are available in various languages. For more information and to book a tour, visit the official website of the cave: (https://www.cuevadeltesoro.com).

Cycling Through Málaga: Málaga's urban landscape and surrounding countryside provide excellent opportunities for cycling enthusiasts. The city is equipped with bike lanes and paths, making it easy to explore both urban and rural areas. Additionally, the nearby Axarquía region offers scenic routes through rolling hills and traditional villages. Bike rentals and guided bike tours are available, with prices starting around €25 for a half-day rental. "Bike & Ride Málaga" offers a variety of cycling tours and rental options, allowing visitors to experience the city's vibrant cycling culture. For more details, visit their website: (https://www.bikeridemalaga.com).

4.12 Guided Tours and Recommended Tour Operators

Málaga's rich history, stunning landscapes, and vibrant culture are best explored with the help of expert tour operators and guides. These professionals offer tailored experiences that provide deep insights into the city's heritage and surroundings. Here are recommended tour operators and guided tours that promise an enriching exploration of Málaga.

Discovering Málaga with "Málaga Local Tours": "Málaga Local Tours" specializes in personalized and immersive city tours. Located in the heart of Málaga, this company offers a variety of guided tours that cover historical landmarks, local cuisine, and cultural hotspots. Their walking tours take visitors through the city's historical center, highlighting key sites such as the Alcazaba Fortress, Málaga Cathedral, and Picasso Museum. Prices for private tours start at approximately €100 for a 2-hour experience. The company prides itself on providing a local perspective, ensuring a unique and engaging exploration of Málaga. For booking and more information, visit their official website: (https://www.malagalocaltours.com).

Exploring Andalusia with "Andalucía Tours": "Andalucía Tours" offers a range of guided tours across the Andalusian region, including Málaga. Their tours include day trips to nearby attractions such as the Alhambra in Granada and the Mezquita in Córdoba. The company provides well-organized excursions with knowledgeable guides who offer in-depth commentary on the historical and cultural significance of each site. Prices vary based on the tour and duration, with full-day tours generally costing around €150 to €200 per person. For an unforgettable Andalusian adventure, visit their website: (https://www.andalucia-tours.com).

Immersive Experiences with "Málaga Culinary Tours": For food lovers, "Málaga Culinary Tours" provides a delightful journey through the city's gastronomic scene. Their guided food tours take visitors to local markets, traditional tapas bars, and gourmet restaurants, offering a taste of Málaga's rich culinary heritage. Tours are designed to introduce participants to local delicacies and cooking traditions, with prices starting around €80 for a 3-hour tour. The company emphasizes authentic experiences and personalized service, making it an ideal choice for food enthusiasts. For more details, visit their website: (https://www.malagaculinarytours.com).

Cultural Insights with "Málaga Art Tours": "Málaga Art Tours" focuses on the city's vibrant art scene, including its rich history in contemporary and classical art. The company offers guided visits to prominent art institutions, such as the Picasso Museum and Centre Pompidou Málaga, as well as lesser-known galleries and art spaces. Tours are led by art experts who provide in-depth analysis and background on the artworks and artists featured. Prices start at €70 for a 2-hour tour. For art enthusiasts seeking an engaging cultural experience, visit their official website: (https://www.malagaarttours.com).

Historical Journeys with "Málaga Heritage Tours": "Málaga Heritage Tours" provides in-depth historical tours that explore the city's rich past. Their tours include visits to historical sites, such as the Alcazaba Fortress and the Roman Theatre, and offer detailed narratives about Málaga's history and its role in Spanish culture. Guided tours are available in multiple languages, with prices starting around €60 for a half-day tour. The company's knowledgeable guides ensure a comprehensive and insightful exploration of Málaga's historical landmarks. For more information and bookings, visit their website: (https://www.malagaheritagetours.com).

CHAPTER 5
PRACTICAL INFORMATION AND GUIDANCE

5.1 Maps and Navigation

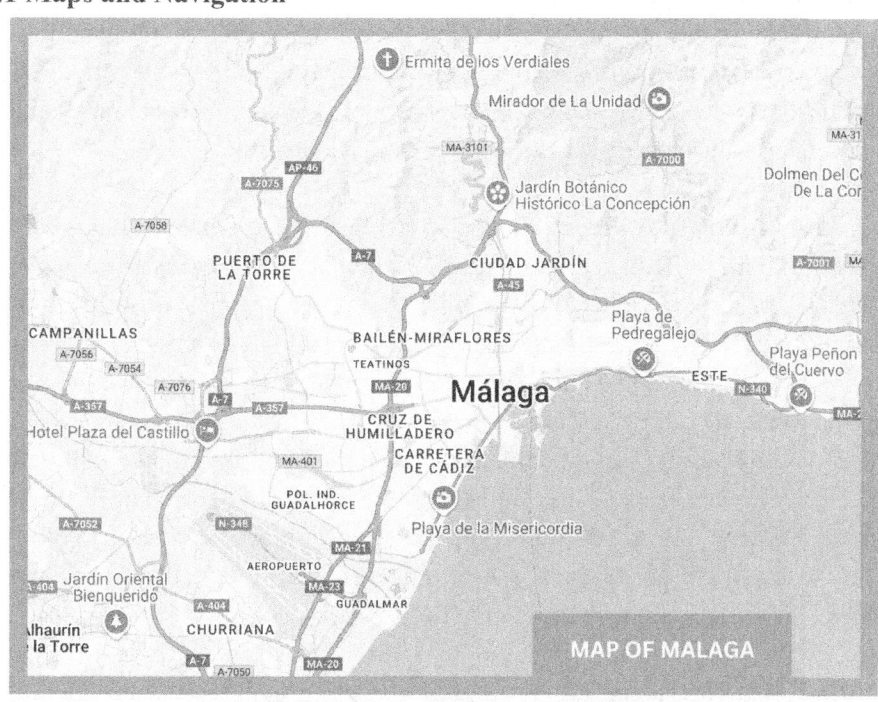

MAP OF MALAGA

SCAN THE QR CODE WITH A DEVICE TO VIEW A COMPREHENSIVE AND LARGER MAP OF MALAGA

Navigating through the vibrant city of Malaga is a delightful experience, enriched by a blend of historical charm and modern conveniences. Whether you are exploring its ancient streets, visiting its numerous museums, or soaking in the sun along its beautiful coastline, having a reliable map is essential. In Malaga, both traditional paper maps and digital maps are readily available to help you make the most of your visit. This guide will walk you through everything you need to know about accessing and using maps in Malaga, ensuring that your journey is as smooth and enjoyable as possible.

The Paper Maps in Malaga: For many travelers, there is something uniquely satisfying about unfolding a paper map and tracing the routes with a finger. In Malaga, tourist maps are widely available at various locations, including tourist information centers, hotels, and even some shops. These maps are typically detailed, highlighting the city's major attractions such as the Alcazaba, the Picasso Museum, and the Cathedral of Malaga. They often include walking routes, public transport information, and tips on the best viewpoints. Visitors can pick up these maps at the main tourist information center located at Plaza de la Marina, a central hub for visitors. The tactile experience of a paper map offers a sense of adventure and allows you to immerse yourself in the city's layout, helping you to navigate without relying on technology.

Digital Maps: Navigating Malaga has become easier than ever with the use of digital maps. Whether you prefer Google Maps, Apple Maps, or other navigation apps, these tools provide real-time directions, traffic updates, and even public transportation schedules. Digital maps are particularly useful for finding specific locations, such as restaurants, shops, or hidden gems, as they offer detailed information including opening hours, reviews, and photos. Travelers can also download offline maps of Malaga, which are invaluable when exploring areas with limited internet access. These offline maps ensure that you can find your way around the city even without a data connection, giving you peace of mind as you explore.

Accessing Digital Maps in Malaga: Accessing digital maps in Malaga is straightforward. Most smartphones come pre-installed with mapping apps, and free Wi-Fi is available at various hotspots throughout the city, including cafes, public squares, and shopping centers. For those who prefer to prepare ahead, maps can be downloaded before arrival, allowing you to plan your itinerary and save points of interest. To enhance your experience, this guidebook includes a

QR code that links directly to a comprehensive digital map of Malaga. By scanning this code, you can access a detailed map that highlights key attractions, walking routes, and insider tips, making your exploration of Malaga both efficient and enjoyable.

Additional Navigation Tips for Exploring Malaga: While maps are essential tools for navigating Malaga, understanding the city's layout can further enhance your experience. Malaga's historic center is compact and pedestrian-friendly, making it ideal for exploring on foot. The main streets, such as Calle Larios, are lined with shops and cafes, while the smaller alleys lead to hidden plazas and historical sites. For longer distances, the city's public transportation system, including buses and the metro, is easy to use and well-integrated with digital mapping apps. Additionally, for those who wish to explore beyond the city center, renting a bicycle or using ride-sharing services can be convenient options, all of which can be navigated seamlessly with digital maps.

Embark on Your Malaga Adventure: With a map in hand, whether paper or digital, you are well-equipped to discover all that Malaga has to offer. The blend of traditional and modern navigation tools ensures that you can enjoy both the timeless charm of the city's streets and the convenience of technology. As you wander through Malaga, the map will not only guide your steps but also enrich your understanding of the city, making your visit an unforgettable experience. For a detailed and interactive exploration, don't forget to scan the QR code in this guidebook to access the comprehensive digital map of Malaga, your ultimate companion on this journey.

5.2 Five Days Itinerary

Malaga offers a blend of rich history, vibrant culture, and stunning landscapes. This five-day itinerary is designed to guide you through the best experiences Malaga has to offer, ensuring that you leave with memories as vivid as the Andalusian sun. From ancient monuments to modern art, culinary delights to coastal escapes, each day unveils a new facet of this captivating city.

Day One: Discovering Malaga's Historic Heart

Begin your journey in the historic center of Malaga, where ancient streets tell stories of a bygone era. Start your day at the Alcazaba, a Moorish fortress-palace that stands as a testament to the city's Islamic past. As you wander through its gardens and courtyards, you'll be transported back to the 11th century, with stunning views of the city below. Next, head to the nearby Roman Theatre, one of the oldest surviving structures in Malaga. The theater, which dates back to the 1st century BC, offers a glimpse into the city's Roman heritage. From there, stroll to the Malaga Cathedral, affectionately known as "La Manquita" or "The One-Armed Lady" due to its unfinished second tower. This Renaissance-style cathedral is a marvel of architecture, with its intricate façades and towering interiors. For lunch, indulge in some local tapas at a nearby restaurant in Plaza de la Merced, a lively square that's perfect for people-watching. In the afternoon, visit the Picasso Museum, which honors Malaga's most famous son, Pablo Picasso. The museum houses an extensive collection of the artist's works, offering insights into his creative genius. End your day with a leisurely walk along Calle Larios, the city's main shopping street, where you can browse through boutiques and enjoy a coffee at one of the many cafes.

Day Two: Art, Culture, and the Modern Malaga
On your second day, immerse yourself in Malaga's contemporary culture. Start at the Centre Pompidou Malaga, a vibrant and colorful museum that's a branch of the famous Paris institution. Here, you'll find an impressive collection of modern and contemporary art, including works by renowned artists like Frida Kahlo and Salvador Dalí. Afterward, visit the nearby Carmen Thyssen Museum, which showcases 19th-century Spanish paintings, with a particular focus on Andalusian art. The museum's collection is a celebration of the region's culture, from its vibrant festivals to its serene landscapes. For lunch, head to the Soho district, Malaga's creative hub. This area is known for its street art, trendy cafes, and innovative cuisine. Afterward, take a stroll through the neighborhood to admire the murals and installations that give this district its unique character. In the afternoon, make your way to the Russian Museum, another branch of a major international institution, where you can explore Russian art from the 15th to the 20th century. The museum's exhibitions often include masterpieces from Russia's most famous artists. Conclude your day with a visit to the Muelle Uno, a modern waterfront complex with shops, restaurants, and stunning views of the port. Enjoy dinner at one of the many seaside restaurants, where you can savor fresh seafood while watching the sunset.

Day Three: Coastal Charms and Scenic Landscapes
Day three is all about exploring the natural beauty surrounding Malaga. Start your day with a visit to the Malaga Botanical Garden, known as La Concepción. This lush, 19th-century garden is a haven of tranquility, with exotic plants,

towering palms, and scenic walking paths. It's the perfect place to enjoy a peaceful morning surrounded by nature. Next, head to the coast for some relaxation at Malagueta Beach, one of the city's most popular beaches. Whether you're looking to swim in the Mediterranean, sunbathe on the golden sands, or simply enjoy a beachside stroll, Malagueta offers a quintessential Malaga experience. There are plenty of chiringuitos (beach bars) where you can grab a refreshing drink or a bite to eat. In the afternoon, take a short drive or bus ride to the nearby town of Rincón de la Victoria. This charming coastal town offers beautiful beaches, a relaxed atmosphere, and the Cueva del Tesoro, one of the few marine caves in Europe that's open to the public. The cave's stunning formations and underground lakes make it a fascinating place to explore. Return to Malaga in the evening and enjoy dinner in the Pedregalejo district, known for its seafood restaurants and lively atmosphere. Here, you can sample traditional dishes like espetos (grilled sardines) while enjoying the sea breeze.

Day Four: Day Trip to the White Villages
On your fourth day, venture beyond Malaga to explore the picturesque white villages (pueblos blancos) of Andalusia. Start with a visit to Mijas, a charming village perched on the mountainside, offering stunning views of the coast below. Mijas is known for its whitewashed houses, narrow streets, and quaint shops selling local crafts. Take a leisurely walk through the village, visiting landmarks like the Chapel of the Virgin of the Rock and the Plaza de Toros, a traditional bullring. If you're feeling adventurous, you can also take a donkey taxi ride through the village, a unique way to experience Mijas. Next, drive to the village of Ronda, one of the most famous white villages in Andalusia. Ronda is known for its dramatic setting atop a deep gorge, which divides the old and new parts of the town. Visit the Puente Nuevo, the iconic bridge that spans the gorge, offering breathtaking views of the surrounding countryside. Explore Ronda's historic sites, including the Moorish King's Palace, the Bullring (one of the oldest in Spain), and the Church of Santa Maria la Mayor. Enjoy lunch at a local restaurant with views of the gorge before returning to Malaga in the late afternoon. In the evening, relax with a glass of wine and some tapas in Malaga's old town, reflecting on your day of exploration.

Day Five: Immersing in Malaga's Local Life
Your final day in Malaga is dedicated to experiencing the city like a local. Start your morning with a visit to the Atarazanas Market, the city's central market, where you can browse through stalls selling fresh produce, meats, cheeses, and

seafood. The market is a feast for the senses and a great place to pick up some local ingredients or snacks. Afterward, take a walk through the Soho district, known for its artistic vibe and creative energy. Explore the street art, galleries, and boutiques that make this area so unique. If you're a fan of contemporary art, you can also visit the CAC Malaga, a contemporary art center that features exhibitions from both established and emerging artists. For lunch, head to the El Palo district, a traditional fishing neighborhood known for its seafood restaurants and laid-back atmosphere. Here, you can enjoy a leisurely meal of fried fish, paella, or other local specialties. In the afternoon, take a stroll along the Paseo del Parque, a beautiful promenade lined with tropical plants and fountains. This is a great place to relax and enjoy the sunshine before heading to the Gibralfaro Castle for one last panoramic view of the city. End your day and your trip with a visit to one of Malaga's traditional taverns, where you can enjoy a glass of sweet Malaga wine and some final tapas. Reflect on the experiences of the past five days and savor the flavors of this vibrant city.

5.3 Essential Packing List

Packing for a trip to Malaga requires a thoughtful balance of essentials that cater to the city's sunny climate, diverse activities, and vibrant culture. Whether you're planning to explore historical sites, relax on the beach, or indulge in local cuisine, having the right items in your suitcase can make your trip more enjoyable and stress-free. This guide offers a comprehensive packing list to ensure you're well-prepared for your Malaga adventure.

Clothing: Malaga enjoys a Mediterranean climate, characterized by hot summers and mild winters, so your wardrobe should reflect the city's sunny disposition. Light, breathable fabrics like cotton and linen are ideal for staying comfortable during the day. Bring along a mix of casual and dressier outfits, as Malaga's atmosphere is generally relaxed but also offers opportunities for more formal dining or cultural events. For daytime exploration, pack comfortable shorts, skirts, and t-shirts or tank tops. A sunhat and sunglasses are must-haves to protect yourself from the strong Andalusian sun. Don't forget to include a lightweight jacket or sweater for cooler evenings, especially if you're visiting in the shoulder seasons of spring or fall. If you plan to visit religious sites, such as the Malaga Cathedral, be sure to pack modest clothing that covers your shoulders and knees out of respect for local customs. A scarf or shawl can be a versatile addition to your packing list, serving both as an accessory and a cover-up.

Footwear: Malaga is a city best explored on foot, with its historic streets, scenic promenades, and lively markets inviting you to wander. Therefore, packing comfortable walking shoes is essential. Opt for sturdy sandals or sneakers that provide good support, especially if you plan to explore sites like the Alcazaba or Gibralfaro Castle, which involve uphill walks. For beach days, bring a pair of flip-flops or sandals that can easily transition from the sand to seaside restaurants. If you're planning on enjoying Malaga's nightlife, a pair of stylish yet comfortable shoes will come in handy for evenings out at tapas bars or flamenco shows.

Beach Essentials: No trip to Malaga would be complete without spending time on its beautiful beaches, so be sure to pack accordingly. A swimsuit is a must, and it's a good idea to bring at least two so you always have a dry one on hand. A lightweight beach towel or sarong can double as a cover-up or be used to relax on the sand. Given Malaga's sunny weather, sunscreen with high SPF is crucial to protect your skin from UV rays. A waterproof sunscreen is particularly useful if you plan on swimming in the Mediterranean. A reusable water bottle is also a smart addition to stay hydrated during your beach days. To fully enjoy the beach experience, consider packing a small beach bag to carry your essentials, such as a book, sunglasses, and snacks. If you're traveling with family or friends, a beach umbrella or pop-up tent can provide some much-needed shade during the hottest parts of the day.

Health and Personal Care: When traveling, it's important to pack health and personal care items that will keep you feeling fresh and safe throughout your trip. In addition to your usual toiletries, include travel-sized versions of essentials like shampoo, conditioner, and body wash. A small first aid kit with band-aids, antiseptic wipes, and any prescription medications is always a wise addition. Given Malaga's warm climate, a good deodorant, insect repellent, and after-sun lotion can be lifesavers. Hand sanitizer and face masks are also useful, especially when using public transport or visiting crowded areas. If you have any specific health concerns, such as allergies, it's advisable to carry a note in Spanish explaining your condition and any necessary medications. This can be particularly helpful if you need to visit a pharmacy or seek medical attention during your stay.

Tech Gear: Technology plays a big role in travel today, and Malaga is no exception. Start by packing a reliable smartphone, not just for communication, but also for navigation, photography, and accessing digital maps of the city. Download offline maps and travel apps before you leave, as they can be incredibly useful if you find yourself without internet access. A portable charger or power bank is essential for keeping your devices charged while you're on the go. If you're planning to capture high-quality photos of Malaga's stunning scenery, consider bringing a compact camera or a GoPro for action shots. Don't forget your adapters and chargers, especially if you're traveling from a country with different plug types. Spain uses the Type C and Type F plug outlets, with a standard voltage of 230V, so be sure your electronics are compatible or pack a voltage converter.

Travel Documents and Money: Having the right travel documents and money management tools is crucial for a stress-free trip to Malaga. Start by ensuring you have a valid passport and, if necessary, a visa. It's also wise to make photocopies of your passport, visa, and any important documents, keeping them separate from the originals in case of loss or theft. A small travel wallet can help keep your documents organized, including your boarding passes, hotel reservations, and any pre-booked tickets for attractions. If you're planning on renting a car, don't forget your driver's license and an international driving permit if required. When it comes to money, Malaga is a modern city with widespread acceptance of credit and debit cards, but it's always useful to carry some euros in cash for small purchases or in case you visit places that don't accept cards. Inform your bank of your travel plans to avoid any issues with card transactions while abroad. A good travel insurance policy is another must-have, providing peace of mind in case of emergencies, whether medical, trip cancellations, or lost luggage.

5.4 Setting Your Travel Budget

Setting a travel budget is a crucial step in planning a memorable and stress-free trip to Malaga. With its sun-drenched beaches, historic landmarks, and lively cultural scene, Malaga offers a wide range of experiences that can fit various budgets. By carefully considering your financial resources and prioritizing your spending, you can enjoy everything this vibrant Andalusian city has to offer without overspending. This guide will help you craft a comprehensive travel budget, covering essential expenses, from accommodation and dining to activities and transportation.

Accommodation: Accommodation is often the most significant part of any travel budget, and Malaga offers a variety of options to suit different financial plans. Whether you're looking for luxury, mid-range comfort, or budget-friendly stays, the city has something for every traveler. For those seeking luxury, Malaga is home to several high-end hotels and resorts, particularly along the coastline and in the city center. Expect to spend more on these options, which often come with premium amenities such as spa services, rooftop pools, and stunning views of the Mediterranean. However, if you're aiming to save money on accommodation, consider booking during the off-season or looking for deals on booking platforms. Mid-range travelers will find a plethora of boutique hotels and guesthouses that offer a comfortable stay at a reasonable price. These establishments often provide a more personalized experience, with unique decor and friendly service, making them a popular choice for visitors looking to balance comfort with cost.

Dining: Malaga is a food lover's paradise, with a culinary scene that ranges from upscale dining to affordable local eateries. Setting a budget for food and drink is essential, especially in a city known for its delicious seafood, tapas, and local wines. If fine dining is on your agenda, Malaga's top restaurants offer exquisite dishes prepared by renowned chefs, often using locally sourced ingredients. While dining at these establishments can be pricey, the experience is well worth the splurge for special occasions. To manage costs, consider having a few lavish meals but balancing them with more affordable options. Mid-range travelers can enjoy Malaga's vibrant tapas culture without breaking the bank. Tapas bars are plentiful in the city, and sharing a variety of small plates is not only a great way to sample local cuisine but also a budget-friendly option. For a more substantial meal, many restaurants offer a "menú del día," a fixed-price lunch menu that includes several courses at a reasonable price.

Transportation: Transportation is another key area to consider when setting your travel budget. Malaga is a compact city with excellent public transport options, so getting around doesn't have to be expensive. For local transportation, Malaga's bus and metro systems are both efficient and affordable. A single bus ticket is inexpensive, and there are various multi-ride and day passes available that can save you money if you plan to use public transport frequently. The metro is a quick and cost-effective way to travel to neighborhoods further from the city center, including the airport. Taxis and ride-sharing services like Uber are also widely available in Malaga, but these can be more expensive, especially for longer trips or during peak times. To save on transport costs, consider walking or cycling, especially in the city center where many attractions are within easy reach.

Activities and Entertainment: Malaga offers a wealth of activities and entertainment options, from exploring historical sites to enjoying the vibrant nightlife. When budgeting for activities, it's essential to consider what experiences are most important to you and how much you're willing to spend on them. For those interested in cultural and historical experiences, Malaga's many museums, such as the Picasso Museum and the Centre Pompidou, offer reasonably priced entry fees, and some even have free admission on certain days. Visiting landmarks like the Alcazaba and Gibralfaro Castle is also affordable and provides stunning views of the city. If you're looking to enjoy the beach and outdoor activities, Malaga's coastline offers plenty of opportunities for sunbathing, swimming, and water sports. Many of these activities are free or low-cost, but if you plan on renting equipment or taking guided tours, be sure to include these expenses in your budget.

5.5 Visa Requirements and Entry Procedures

As you prepare for your visit, understanding the visa requirements and entry procedures is essential for a smooth and stress-free arrival. Whether you are flying into Malaga's international airport, arriving by train, or crossing the border by road, this guide provides all the necessary information to ensure that your entry into Malaga is as seamless as possible.

Visa Requirements for Visiting Malaga: Before embarking on your journey to Malaga, it is crucial to determine whether you need a visa. Spain is a member of the European Union and part of the Schengen Area, which means that citizens of other Schengen countries can enter Malaga without a visa for short stays, typically up to 90 days. For travelers from outside the Schengen Area, the requirements vary depending on your nationality. Citizens of the United States, Canada, Australia, and several other countries do not need a visa for short stays, but it is always advisable to check the most current visa regulations before your trip. If you do require a visa, you will need to apply through the Spanish consulate in your home country. The application process typically involves submitting a completed application form, passport-sized photos, proof of accommodation, travel insurance, and evidence of sufficient funds for your stay. The processing time can vary, so it is recommended to apply well in advance of your planned departure date. Once your visa is approved, it will allow you to travel to Malaga and other Schengen countries within the validity period.

Arriving in Malaga by Air Travel: For most international visitors, arriving in Malaga by air is the most common option. Malaga-Costa del Sol Airport (AGP) is one of the busiest airports in Spain, offering direct flights from numerous destinations across Europe, as well as some long-haul flights from other continents. Upon arrival, passengers will go through passport control, where travelers from non-Schengen countries will need to present their passports and, if required, their visas. The process is usually straightforward, with airport staff guiding you through each step. After clearing passport control, you can collect your luggage and proceed to customs. Travelers with nothing to declare can usually pass through the green channel, while those with items to declare should use the red channel.

Entering Malaga by Train: For those traveling within Europe, arriving in Malaga by train offers a scenic and comfortable alternative to flying. The city is well-connected by Spain's high-speed AVE trains, with direct services from major cities like Madrid, Barcelona, and Seville. If you are arriving from another Schengen country, you will not need to go through any additional border checks, making train travel an efficient and hassle-free option. Upon arrival at Malaga's María Zambrano Station, you will find yourself in the heart of the city, with easy access to public transportation and taxis to reach your accommodation.

Crossing the Border by Road: For those who prefer the flexibility of road travel, entering Malaga by car or bus is also a viable option. Spain shares land borders with Portugal, France, and Andorra, and crossing into Spain from these countries is typically straightforward. If you are driving, ensure that your vehicle's documents are in order, including insurance that covers Spain. When crossing the border, you may be asked to present your passport or national ID card, but there are generally no lengthy procedures involved. For bus travelers, many international bus services connect Malaga with other European cities, offering a comfortable and economical way to travel.

Preparing for a Smooth Arrival in Malaga: Whether you are flying, taking the train, or driving into Malaga, being well-prepared with the necessary documents and understanding the entry procedures will help ensure a smooth and pleasant arrival. It is also advisable to have a copy of your accommodation details and travel itinerary on hand, as these may be requested by immigration officials. By taking the time to familiarize yourself with the visa requirements and entry procedures, you can focus on enjoying all that Malaga has to offer, from its stunning beaches to its rich cultural heritage.

5.6 Safety Tips and Emergency Contacts

Malaga is a relatively safe destination for travelers. However, like any major city, it's important to stay informed and prepared to ensure your visit is both enjoyable and secure. This guide provides essential safety tips and emergency contact information to help you navigate Malaga confidently and handle any unexpected situations with ease.

General Safety Tips: Malaga is known for its friendly locals and welcoming atmosphere, but it's always wise to remain vigilant to ensure your safety. Begin by staying aware of your surroundings, particularly in crowded areas such as markets, bus stations, and tourist hotspots. Petty crime, including pickpocketing, can occur, so it's prudent to keep your belongings close and avoid displaying valuable items like expensive jewelry or large amounts of cash. When exploring the city, use well-lit streets and avoid isolated areas, especially at night. If you're using public transportation or taxis, make sure to choose reputable services. For added security, you might consider using a money belt or a neck pouch to keep important documents and valuables secure. Always inform someone of your whereabouts if you're traveling alone or engaging in activities where you'll be out of reach for a while. This can be particularly important if you plan to venture into less populated areas or go on day trips outside the city.

Emergency Contacts: Knowing how to reach emergency services is crucial during any trip. In Spain, the general emergency number is 112, which connects you to police, medical, and fire services. This number is available 24/7 and is free of charge from any phone. For non-emergency situations or if you need assistance with minor issues, you can contact the local police. If you need to report a lost or stolen item, including passports or credit cards, visit the nearest police station to file a report. If you experience a medical emergency, you can seek assistance at the nearest hospital or clinic. The Hospital Regional Universitario de Malaga, located at Avenida Carlos Haya, 29010 Malaga, is one of the major hospitals in the city. They offer emergency services and can provide comprehensive care if needed. For minor health issues or advice, you may also visit local pharmacies. Many pharmacies in Malaga have staff who can offer basic medical advice and assistance. Look for pharmacies with a "Farmacia" sign, and be sure to check their hours of operation, as some may close for lunch or have varying schedules.

Contacting Your Embassy: If you encounter significant issues such as losing your passport or facing legal troubles, contacting your embassy or consulate can be crucial. The nearest consulate or embassy for your country can provide assistance, including issuing emergency travel documents or offering guidance on legal matters. To find your embassy's contact information, visit their official website or use the directory of embassies and consulates. For U.S. citizens, the nearest U.S. Consulate is located in Malaga at Plaza de la Merced, 5.

Health Precautions: Maintaining good health during your trip involves more than just knowing where to find medical help. It's also about taking proactive steps to avoid illness and injury. Make sure to drink plenty of bottled or filtered water, particularly in hot weather, to stay hydrated. Avoid drinking tap water unless it is confirmed to be safe, and be cautious with street food to prevent foodborne illnesses. Malaga is generally safe, but it's always good to have health insurance that covers medical expenses abroad. Check with your insurance provider before traveling to ensure you have adequate coverage, including emergency medical evacuation if needed. For travelers with specific health concerns, such as allergies or chronic conditions, carry a list of your medications and any medical notes in Spanish. This can help medical professionals provide appropriate care in case of an emergency.

Safety in Specific Situations: Understanding how to handle specific situations can enhance your safety while traveling. If you're involved in a car accident, whether as a driver or passenger, it's essential to remain calm and contact local authorities to file a report. Ensure that you exchange information with other parties involved and take note of any relevant details. In case of natural events such as severe weather, listen to local news and follow any advice or instructions provided by authorities. Malaga occasionally experiences heatwaves, so take precautions such as wearing appropriate clothing, using sunscreen, and avoiding prolonged exposure to the sun.

5.7 Currency Exchange and Banking Services

Málaga offers a blend of modern conveniences and traditional charm, making it an appealing destination for tourists. Understanding the currency, banking options, and money management in Málaga is essential for a smooth travel experience. The city uses the Euro (€) as its official currency, and visitors will find various banking services and currency exchange facilities to cater to their financial needs.

Currency in Málaga: The Euro is the standard currency used in Málaga, as well as throughout Spain and most of Europe. As a visitor, it is crucial to familiarize yourself with the current exchange rate between your home currency and the Euro to budget effectively. Currency exchange rates can fluctuate, so it's advisable to check the latest rates before traveling. While credit and debit cards are widely accepted in hotels, restaurants, and shops, having some cash on hand is useful, especially for smaller purchases and in more remote areas.

Banking Services in Málaga: Málaga boasts a range of banking services tailored to both locals and visitors. The city is home to several reputable banks that offer a variety of financial services, including currency exchange, cash withdrawals, and general banking needs. Understanding these options can help you manage your finances efficiently during your stay.

Banco Santander: Banco Santander is one of Spain's largest and most well-known banks, with a significant presence in Málaga. The bank provides a wide array of banking services, including foreign currency exchange, ATMs, and assistance with international transactions. For visitors, the branch located at Calle Larios, Málaga's main shopping street, is particularly convenient. This central location allows easy access to essential banking services, whether you need to withdraw cash or exchange currency.

BBVA: BBVA, another major banking institution, is known for its excellent customer service and comprehensive banking solutions. In Málaga, BBVA operates several branches, including one on Avenida de Andalucía. This branch offers various services such as currency exchange, ATM access, and personal banking assistance. The bank's focus on customer convenience makes it a practical choice for tourists needing banking services.

CaixaBank: CaixaBank is a prominent player in Málaga's banking sector, providing a range of financial services to both locals and visitors. The branch located at Plaza de la Constitución, right in the heart of the city, offers easy access to currency exchange and ATM services. The modern facilities and customer-focused approach ensure that visitors can handle their financial transactions smoothly and efficiently.

Bankia: Bankia, now integrated into CaixaBank, continues to offer reliable banking services in Málaga. Its branch at Calle Alcazabilla is well-situated for tourists exploring the city. The bank provides essential services such as currency exchange and ATM access, with a strong emphasis on customer support. This branch's central location makes it an accessible option for managing your finances while enjoying Málaga.

Sabadell Bank: Sabadell Bank, located on Calle Martínez Campos, is another viable option for visitors. Known for its dependable banking services, Sabadell Bank offers currency exchange and ATM facilities. The branch's central location ensures that tourists have easy access to financial services, whether they are in need of cash withdrawals or exchanging their home currency.

Currency Exchange Facilities: In addition to bank branches, Málaga offers various currency exchange facilities that can be useful for visitors. Exchange bureaus are scattered throughout the city, including at major transportation hubs like Málaga Airport and the bus station. These locations are convenient for travelers arriving in the city and needing immediate currency conversion. One well-regarded bureau is Global Exchange, which operates at Málaga Airport. This bureau provides competitive exchange rates and is open daily, catering to travelers arriving at various times. The central location ensures easy access for those arriving by air. Another notable option is Change Group, located in the city center at Plaza de la Merced. This bureau offers convenient services for tourists needing to exchange currency while exploring the city. With its strategic location, visitors can easily manage their financial needs during their stay in Málaga.

5.8 Language, Communication and Useful Phrases

As you prepare to immerse yourself in the vibrant culture of Malaga, understanding the local language and communication customs will greatly enhance your experience. Spanish is the official language of Malaga, and while many people in the city speak some English, especially in tourist areas, learning a few key phrases in Spanish can go a long way in making your interactions smoother and more enjoyable. This guide will provide you with essential information on language, communication tips, and useful phrases to help you connect with the locals and fully embrace the charm of Malaga.

The Role of Spanish in Malaga's Daily Life: Spanish, or Castellano as it is known in Spain, is the language spoken by the vast majority of Malaga's residents. It is a melodic and expressive language, deeply intertwined with the city's culture and traditions. While English is commonly spoken in hotels, restaurants, and tourist attractions, especially in the more popular areas, you will find that many locals appreciate it when visitors make an effort to speak Spanish, even if it is just a few words. In more traditional neighborhoods and markets, Spanish is the predominant language, and knowing a bit of the local tongue can open doors to more authentic experiences.

Useful Phrases for Navigating Malaga: To help you get started, here are some useful phrases that can be handy during your visit to Malaga. When greeting someone, you can say "Hola" (Hello) or "Buenos días" (Good morning). If you want to ask for help or directions, you can use "¿Dónde está…?" (Where is…?) followed by the place you are looking for, such as "el Museo Picasso" (the Picasso Museum). To express gratitude, "Gracias" (Thank you) or "Muchas gracias" (Thank you very much) will be appreciated. If you need assistance in a restaurant or café, "¿Puede ayudarme?" (Can you help me?) or "¿La cuenta, por favor?" (The bill, please?) are essential phrases. For those interested in shopping, "¿Cuánto cuesta esto?" (How much does this cost?) will come in handy.

Communicating with Locals: While many people in Malaga have a basic understanding of English, especially in tourist-heavy areas, it's worth noting that using Spanish, even if imperfectly, can enrich your interactions with locals. Spaniards are known for their warmth and friendliness, and making an effort to speak their language often leads to more engaging conversations and helpful responses. Simple gestures like saying "Por favor" (Please) and "Disculpe" (Excuse me) can go a long way in ensuring respectful and pleasant interactions.

Digital Tools to Aid Communication: In addition to learning key phrases, digital tools can be incredibly useful for overcoming language barriers.

Translation apps like Google Translate can provide quick translations and even offer pronunciation help, which can be especially useful in situations where you need to communicate more complex ideas. Many of these apps also have offline modes, which can be beneficial if you find yourself in an area with limited internet connectivity.

Cultural Nuances and Non-Verbal Communication: Understanding cultural nuances is also important for effective communication. In Spain, physical proximity and gestures play a significant role in conversation. A handshake is common when meeting someone, but closer friends and family may greet with a kiss on each cheek. Maintaining eye contact is a sign of attentiveness and respect. Being mindful of these social norms can enhance your interactions and help you navigate social situations with ease.

Navigating Malaga's Multilingual Environment: Malaga is a cosmopolitan city with a diverse population, so you might encounter a variety of languages spoken, especially in tourist areas. However, Spanish remains the primary language of communication. Embracing the local language will not only make your visit more immersive but also allow you to connect with the culture on a deeper level. For those traveling with Spanish speakers, having a bilingual companion can be advantageous, but even solo travelers will find that basic Spanish skills significantly enhance their experience.

Enhancing Your Travel Experience: Equipped with basic Spanish phrases and an understanding of local communication practices, you will be better prepared to explore all that Malaga has to offer. From charming tapas bars to bustling markets, knowing how to navigate the language and cultural nuances will allow you to fully enjoy your visit and create memorable experiences. Whether you're ordering a delicious meal, asking for directions, or engaging with local residents, a little effort in learning the language can make your journey in Malaga both enriching and enjoyable.

5.9 Shopping in Malaga

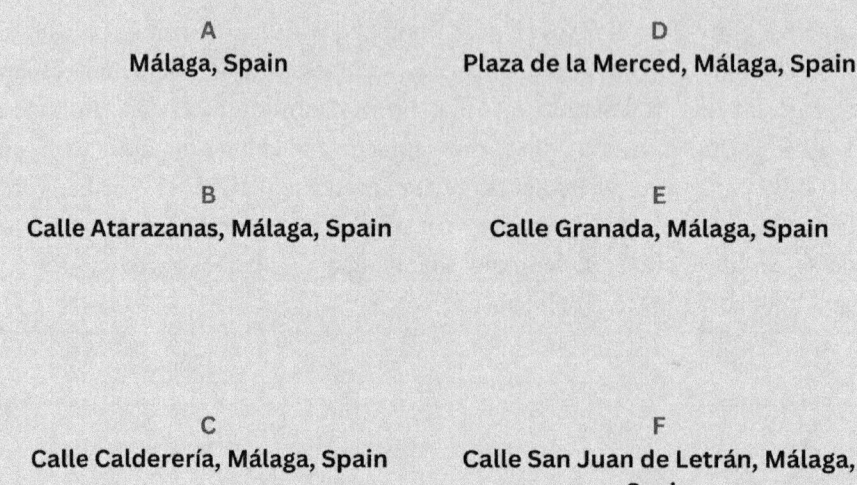

Directions from Málaga, Spain to Calle San Juan de Letrán, Málaga, Spain

A
Málaga, Spain

B
Calle Atarazanas, Málaga, Spain

C
Calle Calderería, Málaga, Spain

D
Plaza de la Merced, Málaga, Spain

E
Calle Granada, Málaga, Spain

F
Calle San Juan de Letrán, Málaga, Spain

Málaga offers an exciting array of shopping opportunities. From charming boutique stores to unique antique shops, the city caters to diverse tastes and interests. Whether you're hunting for stylish fashion pieces, one-of-a-kind antiques, or local souvenirs, Málaga has a shopping destination for every visitor. Here's a comprehensive look at distinctive shopping options you can find in Málaga, all of which are prominently featured on Google Maps.

Boutique Shopping at Mercado de Atarazanas: The Mercado de Atarazanas, located on Calle Atarazanas, stands as one of Málaga's most iconic shopping venues. This bustling market, housed in a historic 14th-century building, offers a vibrant shopping experience where visitors can explore a variety of goods. The market is renowned for its fresh produce, local delicacies, and artisanal products. Here, shoppers can find an array of gourmet foods, from cured hams and cheeses to fresh seafood and exotic fruits. Prices at the Mercado de Atarazanas vary depending on the products, but you can expect to pay around €5 to €20 for local specialty items. The market is open Monday through Saturday from 8:00 AM to 3:00 PM. It's conveniently located in the city center, making it easily accessible by foot or public transportation. The lively atmosphere and historic ambiance make this market a must-visit for anyone looking to experience the culinary and cultural essence of Málaga.

Vintage Finds at Vintage & Chic: For those with a penchant for vintage fashion, Vintage & Chic, situated on Calle Calderería, offers a treasure trove of classic clothing and accessories. This boutique specializes in high-quality vintage apparel from the 20th century, including elegant dresses, retro jackets, and unique jewelry. Prices here range from €30 to €150, depending on the rarity and condition of the items. Vintage & Chic operates from Tuesday to Saturday, with opening hours from 11:00 AM to 7:00 PM. The store's cozy and eclectic interior makes for an enjoyable shopping experience, and its central location ensures easy access for visitors exploring the city's cultural attractions.

Antiques at Anticuarium: Anticuarium, located on Plaza de la Merced, is a haven for antique enthusiasts. This charming store specializes in a wide range of antique items, including furniture, artworks, and collectibles. Visitors can browse through exquisite pieces such as ornate mirrors, vintage ceramics, and rare coins. Prices at Anticuarium vary significantly, from €50 for smaller collectibles to several thousand euros for larger furniture pieces. The shop is open Monday through Saturday from 10:00 AM to 6:00 PM. Situated in one of

Málaga's most picturesque squares, Anticuarium is a delightful stop for those interested in finding unique historical artifacts. The square itself is also a great place to enjoy a leisurely stroll after shopping.

Local Crafts at La Casa del Vino: La Casa del Vino, located on Calle Granada, is a specialty store dedicated to showcasing local wines and crafts. Here, visitors can purchase a selection of fine Spanish wines, local olive oils, and handcrafted pottery. The store is known for its excellent selection of regional products, which make perfect souvenirs for those looking to bring a taste of Málaga home. Wine prices start around €10 per bottle, while handcrafted pottery items range from €20 to €50. La Casa del Vino is open daily from 10:00 AM to 8:00 PM, making it a convenient stop for both early and late shoppers. Its location near the historic center means that it is easily accessible and well-suited for combining a shopping trip with a tour of nearby attractions.

Souvenirs at El Rincón del Arte: El Rincón del Arte, found on Calle San Juan de Letrán, offers a delightful selection of souvenirs and local artwork. This store features handmade crafts, traditional Spanish ceramics, and a variety of souvenirs that capture the essence of Málaga. Visitors can find items such as colorful tilework, local paintings, and charming figurines. Prices here range from €10 to €60, depending on the item and its intricacy. The shop operates from Tuesday to Sunday, from 10:00 AM to 6:00 PM. Its location in the historic part of the city makes it a convenient spot for picking up mementos after exploring Málaga's cultural landmarks.

5.10 Health and Wellness Centers

Málaga is an ideal destination for those seeking relaxation and rejuvenation. The city is home to a variety of health and wellness centers that cater to diverse needs, from luxurious spas and fitness centers to holistic healing retreats. Each establishment offers a unique approach to wellness, ensuring that visitors can find the perfect place to unwind, revitalize, and enhance their well-being.

Luxury Rejuvenation at Hammam Al Ándalus: Hammam Al Ándalus, situated on Calle Viento, provides an enchanting journey into the world of traditional Arabic baths. This luxurious wellness center offers an authentic hammam experience, combining ancient rituals with modern comfort. Visitors can indulge in a range of treatments, including soothing massages, exfoliating scrubs, and aromatic baths. The serene atmosphere, complete with intricate tilework and calming water features, creates a peaceful retreat from the hustle and bustle of city life. The center operates daily from 10:00 AM to 10:00 PM, making it convenient for both daytime and evening visits. Prices for treatments vary depending on the service, with standard hammam experiences starting around €40. Hammam Al Ándalus is centrally located, allowing easy access for those exploring Málaga's cultural and historical landmarks.

Holistic Healing at Centro de Terapias Integrativas: For those seeking a holistic approach to wellness, Centro de Terapias Integrativas on Avenida de Andalucía offers a comprehensive range of therapies aimed at promoting overall health. This center specializes in integrative treatments, including acupuncture, reflexology, and energy healing. Their team of experienced practitioners focuses on personalized care, tailoring each session to meet the specific needs of the individual. The center operates from Monday to Friday, from 9:00 AM to 6:00 PM, and is open on Saturdays by appointment. Prices for therapies start at approximately €50 per session. The welcoming environment and expert staff make Centro de Terapias Integrativas a preferred choice for visitors looking to explore alternative health practices.

Fitness and Relaxation at Metropolitan Málaga: Metropolitan Málaga, located on Calle Don Alonso, is a premier fitness and wellness center offering a comprehensive range of services designed to promote physical health and relaxation. The facility features state-of-the-art gym equipment, group fitness classes, and a tranquil spa area. Visitors can take advantage of various classes such as yoga, pilates, and spinning, or opt for personal training sessions to achieve their fitness goals. In addition to its fitness offerings, Metropolitan Málaga boasts a luxurious spa with services including massages, facials, and hydrotherapy treatments. The center is open Monday through Friday from 7:00 AM to 10:00 PM and on weekends from 9:00 AM to 8:00 PM. Membership options and day passes are available, with prices starting around €15 for a day pass. Its central location ensures easy access for visitors wanting to integrate fitness and wellness into their Málaga experience.

Wellness and Beauty at Hotel Vincci Selección Posada del Patio: The Hotel Vincci Selección Posada del Patio, located on Calle Garcilaso, combines luxury accommodation with an exceptional wellness experience. The hotel's spa, known for its elegant design and high-quality services, offers a range of treatments including massages, body scrubs, and facial therapies. Guests can enjoy the spa's serene environment, complete with modern facilities and skilled therapists. The spa is open daily from 10:00 AM to 8:00 PM, and treatment prices vary depending on the service, with options starting around €60. In addition to spa services, the hotel provides a wellness-focused stay, including access to its fitness center and relaxing pool area. The Vincci Selección Posada del Patio's location in the heart of Málaga makes it a convenient choice for those seeking a luxurious wellness experience in a central setting.

Rejuvenation at Spa & Fitness Center Málaga: The Spa & Fitness Center Málaga, located on Calle de la Orotava, offers a versatile range of wellness services designed to cater to both relaxation and fitness needs. The center features a modern gym, complete with the latest fitness equipment, as well as a full-service spa offering massages, thermal therapies, and beauty treatments. The comprehensive approach ensures that visitors can address their physical fitness while also enjoying rejuvenating spa experiences. The center operates Monday through Saturday from 8:00 AM to 9:00 PM and is closed on Sundays. Day passes and membership options are available, with prices starting at €20 for a day pass. The facility's convenient location and extensive service offerings make it an excellent choice for visitors seeking both fitness and relaxation during their stay in Málaga.

5.11 Useful Websites, Mobile Apps and Online Resources

In the modern era of travel, digital resources play an indispensable role in planning and enhancing your visit to Malaga. With a plethora of websites, mobile apps, and online tools available, travelers can access real-time information, navigate the city with ease, and discover a wealth of experiences at their fingertips. This guide delves into invaluable digital resources that can significantly enrich your Malaga experience, providing detailed insights into each platform's unique services and functionalities.

TripAdvisor: TripAdvisor stands out as a comprehensive platform for travelers seeking detailed reviews and recommendations. Its website and mobile app are invaluable resources for exploring Malaga. Users can access a wide range of information, including detailed reviews from fellow travelers, ratings, and photos of hotels, restaurants, and attractions. The platform allows you to compare prices, make reservations, and even book tours directly through the app. Whether you're looking for a charming restaurant in the city center or a comfortable hotel near the beach, TripAdvisor provides extensive user-generated content that helps in making informed decisions and discovering hidden gems throughout Malaga.

Malaga City Official Website: The Malaga City Official Website is a vital resource for obtaining up-to-date information about the city's attractions, events, and practical details. This site offers comprehensive information about local landmarks, cultural events, and public services. Visitors can access details about ongoing festivals, museum openings, and public transportation schedules. The website also provides practical information about city regulations, emergency contacts, and accessibility services, making it an essential tool for planning your visit and staying informed about local happenings.

Eventbrite: Eventbrite is an excellent app for discovering local events and activities during your stay in Malaga. The platform allows users to browse a diverse range of events, from music concerts and theater performances to food festivals and art exhibitions. By using Eventbrite, you can explore what's happening in Malaga on specific dates, read event descriptions, and purchase tickets directly through the app. This resource is particularly useful for travelers looking to immerse themselves in the local cultural scene and find unique experiences that might not be listed in traditional travel guides.

Trafico: For those driving in Malaga, the Trafico app provides essential information about traffic conditions and parking availability. This app, managed by the Spanish Directorate-General for Traffic, offers real-time updates on traffic situations, road closures, and parking regulations. It can be particularly useful for navigating the city's often busy streets and finding suitable parking options. Trafico also provides information on traffic fines and regulations, ensuring that you are well-informed about driving rules and can avoid potential issues during your visit.

5.12 Internet Access and Connectivity

Málaga offers various options for internet access and connectivity. The city's infrastructure supports a range of services designed to keep visitors connected, from public Wi-Fi hotspots to local SIM cards. Understanding these options can enhance your travel experience and ensure seamless connectivity throughout your stay.

Public Wi-Fi Hotspots: : Málaga provides an array of public Wi-Fi hotspots across the city, offering free internet access in many key locations. These hotspots are commonly found in popular areas such as parks, public squares, and shopping districts. For instance, Plaza de la Constitución and Parque de Málaga are equipped with free Wi-Fi, allowing visitors to connect while enjoying these iconic spots. Additionally, many cafes and restaurants in the city offer complimentary Wi-Fi to patrons, making it easy to access the internet while dining or relaxing. To connect to these public networks, simply search for available Wi-Fi connections on your device and select the relevant network. Some hotspots may require you to enter a password or accept terms of use, which is typically provided by the establishment or displayed on a welcome page. Public Wi-Fi is a convenient option, though it's wise to use secure networks and avoid accessing sensitive information to protect your personal data.

Local SIM Cards and Mobile Data: : For more robust and flexible internet access, purchasing a local SIM card is a practical choice. Several telecommunications providers in Málaga offer prepaid SIM cards with data plans suitable for short-term visitors. Companies such as Vodafone, Movistar, and Orange have retail outlets throughout the city, including at Málaga Airport, where you can purchase and activate a SIM card upon arrival. Local SIM cards provide a range of data packages, from small plans for light browsing to larger ones for extensive use. Prices vary based on the data allowance and duration, with options typically starting around €10 for a basic plan. Once you have your SIM card, inserting it into your unlocked phone will allow you to access mobile data and make calls within Spain and across Europe. This option is ideal for travelers who need constant internet access and prefer not to rely on public Wi-Fi.

Internet Cafés: : Internet cafés continue to be a valuable resource for travelers who may not have their own devices or prefer a more traditional setup for internet access. In Málaga, several internet cafés provide computers with internet access, along with printing and scanning services. These establishments cater to both tourists and locals, offering a comfortable environment to browse the web, check emails, or perform other online tasks. One such popular spot is Café y Letras, located in the city center. This café offers a cozy atmosphere where you can access the internet while enjoying a coffee. Another option is Cyber Café Málaga, situated near the main shopping areas. Both venues offer competitive rates for internet use, typically charging by the hour. Using an internet café can be particularly useful if you need to print documents or require a more private space to work.

Accommodation Wi-Fi: : Many hotels, hostels, and vacation rentals in Málaga provide free Wi-Fi as part of their amenities. This service is generally included in the room rate, allowing guests to connect to the internet from the comfort of their accommodation. Most establishments offer strong and reliable connections, though the quality can vary depending on the location and type of property. When booking your stay, it's advisable to check the details regarding Wi-Fi availability to ensure it meets your needs. Higher-end hotels often provide premium internet services with faster speeds and greater bandwidth, which can be beneficial for business travelers or those who require a stable connection for streaming and video calls. For those staying in private rentals, communicating with the host about Wi-Fi access and speed before arrival can help avoid any connectivity issues during your stay.

Co-Working Spaces: : For digital nomads or business travelers, Málaga offers several co-working spaces equipped with high-speed internet and a range of professional amenities. These spaces provide a productive environment for working remotely and are an excellent alternative to cafés or public Wi-Fi. Co-working spaces often include additional services such as meeting rooms, printing facilities, and networking events, making them ideal for professionals needing a more structured work setting. One prominent co-working space in Málaga is La Casa del Humo, located in the historic center. This modern facility offers fast internet, comfortable workstations, and various membership options. Another option is WeWork, which has a location in the city, providing flexible workspaces and amenities designed for productivity. Co-working spaces typically offer day passes or monthly memberships, with prices starting around €20 per day. These spaces are perfect for travelers who need reliable internet access and a professional environment while away from home.

5.13 Visitor Centers and Tourist Assistance

Exploring a new city can be an exhilarating experience, but it often requires guidance and support to make the most of your visit. Malaga, a vibrant city on Spain's Costa del Sol, offers a range of visitor centers and tourist assistance services designed to help travelers navigate its rich cultural landscape and ensure a memorable stay. These centers provide valuable information, support, and services to enhance your travel experience, whether you're seeking guidance on attractions, local customs, or practical travel advice.

Malaga Tourist Information Office: One of the most important resources for visitors is the Malaga Tourist Information Office, strategically located in the heart of the city. Situated at Plaza de la Marina, 11, this central office is an excellent starting point for anyone new to Malaga. The friendly staff here provide comprehensive information about local attractions, accommodations, and dining options. They offer free maps and brochures detailing the city's landmarks, events, and transportation options. Additionally, they can assist with booking guided tours, providing recommendations based on your interests, and answering any questions you may have about navigating Malaga.

Tourist Information Office at Malaga-Costa del Sol Airport: For travelers arriving by air, the Tourist Information Office at Malaga-Costa del Sol Airport is a valuable resource. Located in Terminal 3 of the airport, this office is open daily and offers a range of services to assist visitors as soon as they land. Here, you can obtain maps of the city, learn about transportation options to and from the airport, and get information on nearby accommodations. The staff can help with currency exchange, provide advice on local customs, and offer tips on must-see attractions in and around Malaga.

Malaga City Hall Tourist Office: The Tourist Office located within the Malaga City Hall, situated at Plaza del Ayuntamiento, 1, provides a more in-depth look at the city's cultural and historical aspects. This office is ideal for visitors interested in learning about Malaga's rich heritage and local traditions. The staff here can provide detailed explanations of historical sites, recommend cultural events, and offer insights into the city's unique festivals and celebrations. Additionally, they can assist with information on local guided tours and cultural activities that offer a deeper understanding of Malaga's history and customs.

Museo Carmen Thyssen Malaga: For those particularly interested in art and culture, the Tourist Information Office at Museo Carmen Thyssen Malaga, located at Calle Compañía, 10, offers specialized assistance. This museum is not only a major cultural attraction but also serves as a resource for visitors seeking information about Malaga's art scene. The staff can provide details about current exhibitions, offer insights into the museum's collection, and recommend other cultural venues and events in the city. This office is particularly helpful for art lovers looking to explore Malaga's vibrant artistic heritage.

Malaga Port Tourist Information Center: The Malaga Port Tourist Information Center, located near the cruise terminal at Muelle 2, is an essential resource for travelers arriving by sea. This center caters to cruise ship passengers and other maritime visitors, offering information on local excursions, shore activities, and port facilities. The staff can assist with booking local tours, provide recommendations for dining and shopping in the port area, and offer advice on exploring the city from the waterfront. They also provide information on transportation options from the port to various parts of Malaga, making it easier for visitors to plan their stay.

Special Services and Assistance: In addition to the services provided by these visitor centers, Malaga offers several special assistance programs to enhance your travel experience. Many centers offer multilingual staff to cater to international visitors, ensuring that language barriers do not hinder your exploration of the city. They also provide accessible services for travelers with disabilities, including information on accessible attractions, transportation, and accommodations. For those seeking personalized experiences, some tourist offices can arrange private tours, special events, or tailored itineraries based on your interests. Whether you're interested in exploring the city's historic sites, enjoying its culinary delights, or discovering its natural beauty, the staff at these centers can help create a customized experience that meets your needs.

CHAPTER 6
GASTRONOMIC DELIGHTS

6.1 Dining Options and Top Restaurants

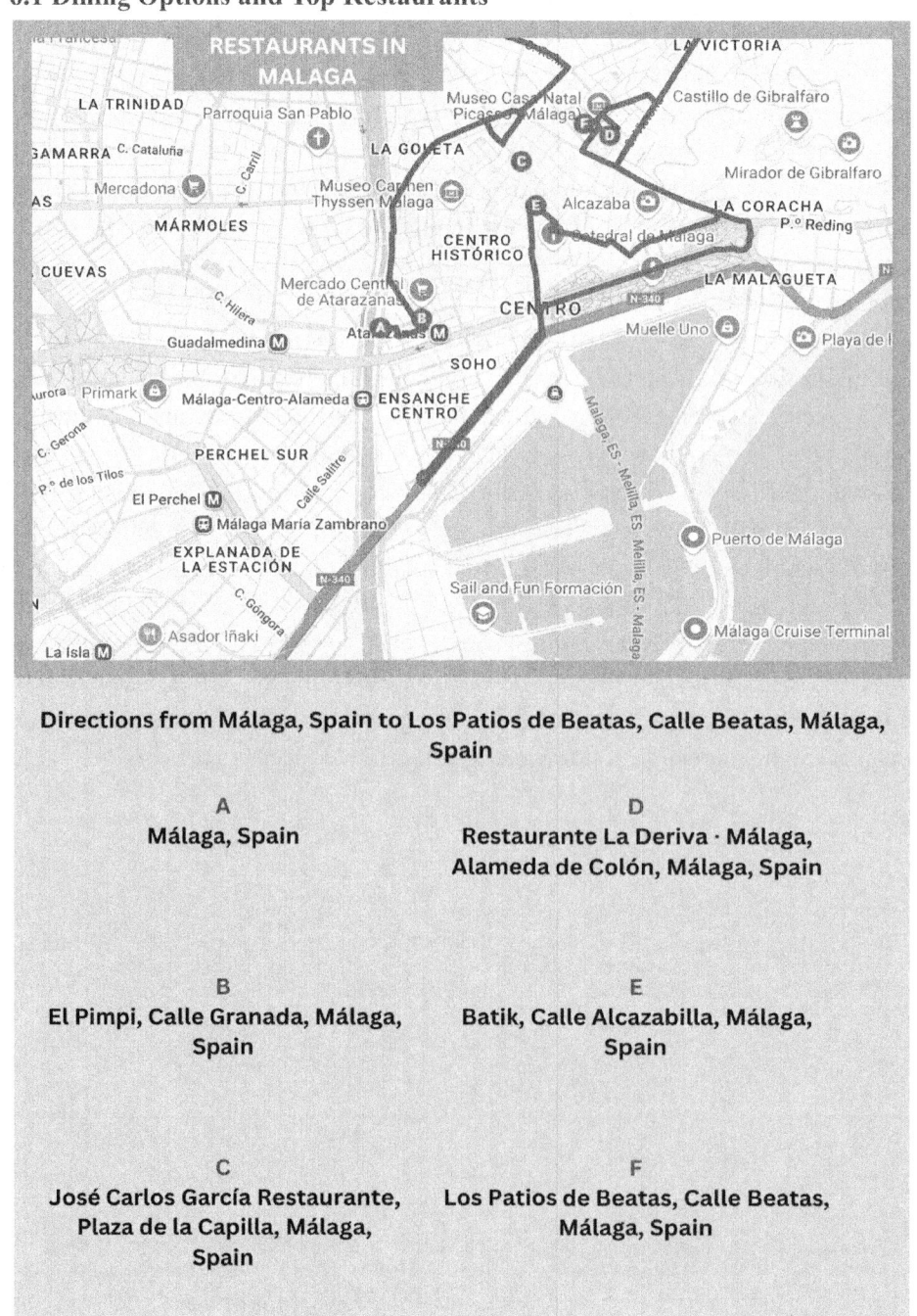

Directions from Málaga, Spain to Los Patios de Beatas, Calle Beatas, Málaga, Spain

A
Málaga, Spain

D
Restaurante La Deriva · Málaga, Alameda de Colón, Málaga, Spain

B
El Pimpi, Calle Granada, Málaga, Spain

E
Batik, Calle Alcazabilla, Málaga, Spain

C
José Carlos García Restaurante, Plaza de la Capilla, Málaga, Spain

F
Los Patios de Beatas, Calle Beatas, Málaga, Spain

Málaga, a vibrant city on Spain's sun-soaked Costa del Sol, is not only known for its historic sites and coastal beauty but also for its incredible culinary scene. Whether you're in the mood for traditional Andalusian fare or modern gastronomic experiences, Málaga's dining options cater to all palates. Below, we explore exceptional dining experiences, detailing their unique flavors, ambiance, and practical information that every visitor will need to know.

El Pimpi: Tucked into the heart of Málaga's old town, El Pimpi is more than just a restaurant; it's a cultural landmark. This iconic venue, located near the Roman Theatre and Alcazaba fortress, offers a true Andalusian experience, serving traditional tapas and full-course meals that embody the region's culinary heritage. The menu highlights local ingredients with dishes like "berenjenas con miel" (fried eggplant with honey), succulent jamón Ibérico, and fresh seafood straight from the Mediterranean. You'll also find local wines, including the famous sweet Málaga wine, which pairs perfectly with their offerings. The atmosphere at El Pimpi is equally enchanting, with walls covered in photographs of famous patrons and a charming outdoor terrace. Prices are moderate, with tapas ranging from €4 to €8, while mains can cost between €15 and €30. El Pimpi opens at 12:00 p.m. and closes around midnight, making it an excellent option for both lunch and dinner.

Restaurante José Carlos García: For those seeking a refined, avant-garde dining experience, Restaurante José Carlos García is a must-visit. Situated in the lively Muelle Uno area of Málaga's port, this Michelin-starred restaurant offers a luxurious escape into creative Spanish cuisine. Chef José Carlos García's tasting menu is a journey through flavors, textures, and artful presentations, with a focus on local and seasonal ingredients. Expect dishes like red shrimp tartare with beetroot and a roasted pigeon with caramelized onions. The prices reflect the high-end experience, with the tasting menu priced around €135 per person, and wine pairings available for an additional €65. The restaurant has an elegant, minimalist interior that mirrors its culinary precision. It opens for dinner service from 8:30 p.m. to 11:00 p.m., offering an intimate atmosphere for a special evening. Due to its popularity, reservations are highly recommended.

La Deriva: Located along the Guadalmedina River, La Deriva offers a fresh take on Mediterranean cuisine by blending traditional flavors with modern techniques. This restaurant is known for its inventive approach to familiar dishes, such as octopus with black garlic aioli and slow-cooked oxtail ravioli. Its extensive wine list features an array of local and international selections, catering to both casual diners and wine connoisseurs. Prices at La Deriva are moderate, with tapas and starters costing between €5 and €12, while main courses are typically priced between €15 and €25. The restaurant's contemporary, sleek décor makes it a trendy yet relaxed space, perfect for both lunch and dinner. La Deriva is open from 1:00 p.m. to 4:30 p.m. for lunch and from 8:00 p.m. to 11:30 p.m. for dinner, providing plenty of opportunities to enjoy their culinary fusion.

Batik: For an unforgettable dining experience with a view, Batik offers one of the most stunning settings in Málaga. Perched atop the Alcazaba Premium Hostel, Batik overlooks the city's historic landmarks, including the Alcazaba fortress and the Cathedral. The restaurant serves a menu that combines Spanish flavors with international influences, featuring dishes like tuna tataki, lamb tagine, and vegetarian-friendly quinoa salads. Their cocktails are equally notable, with refreshing options like mojitos and gin and tonics that are perfect for sipping while enjoying the panoramic vistas. Batik's prices are fairly reasonable, with starters around €8 to €12 and main dishes between €15 and €25. The rooftop ambiance, complete with soft lighting and chic furnishings, elevates the dining experience, making it ideal for a romantic evening or a relaxed night with friends. Batik opens from 1:30 p.m. to 3:30 p.m. for lunch and reopens for dinner service from 8:00 p.m. to midnight. It's advisable to make a reservation, especially for the evening hours, as the rooftop tends to fill up quickly.

Los Patios de Beatas: Wine enthusiasts will find their haven at Los Patios de Beatas, a beautifully restored building in the heart of Málaga's city center. This restaurant and wine bar focuses on pairing excellent Spanish wines with high-quality dishes, many of which are influenced by local and regional traditions. The menu is designed to complement the wine selection, offering tapas such as grilled prawns with saffron aioli, cured meats, and artisanal cheeses. Main dishes feature fresh seafood, meats, and vegetarian options, each crafted with care to highlight the flavors of the wines on offer. Prices are moderate to high depending on the selection, with tapas starting at around €5 and main courses typically ranging from €18 to €35. The real highlight of Los Patios de Beatas is the wine-tasting experience, where knowledgeable staff guide visitors through the nuances of Spanish wine, offering a range of tastings from €20 to €50 depending on the selection. The restaurant is open from 1:00

p.m. to 11:00 p.m., and reservations are recommended, especially for wine tastings and weekends.

6.2 Traditional Andalusian Cuisine

Dining in Málaga is more than just eating; it's a way to connect with the vibrant soul of Andalusia. Visitors will find that each dish tells a story—of the sun-soaked fields, the bustling fish markets, and the pride of the people who have perfected these recipes over generations. From refreshing gazpachos to rich stews, traditional Andalusian cuisine offers an unforgettable sensory journey. Below are some of the most iconic dishes, where to find them, and tips for making the most of your culinary adventure.

Gazpachuelo: One of the most traditional and comforting dishes in Málaga is gazpachuelo, a humble soup that originated from the fishermen along the coast. Made with a base of fish stock, egg yolk, olive oil, and potatoes, it is both warming and rich, embodying the flavors of the sea. Unlike the famous cold gazpacho, gazpachuelo is served hot, making it perfect for cooler days or as a hearty meal after a long day exploring the city. To truly experience the authenticity of gazpachuelo, head to El Refectorium Catedral, located near the iconic Málaga Cathedral. This local favorite serves a beautiful version of the dish, made fresh daily. Prices for a bowl of gazpachuelo start at €10, making it a reasonably priced option for anyone wanting to taste a true slice of Málaga's culinary heritage. The restaurant opens from 1:00 p.m. to 4:00 p.m. for lunch, and again from 8:00 p.m. to midnight for dinner, giving visitors plenty of time to indulge.

Porra Antequerana: For those seeking something more robust than the typical gazpacho, porra antequerana is a must-try dish. This thicker, creamier variation of cold tomato soup originates from the nearby town of Antequera, but it's widely embraced in Málaga. Made from tomatoes, bread, olive oil, garlic, and topped with hard-boiled eggs and cured ham, it is a dish that balances richness with the freshness of Andalusian produce.

Espeto de Sardinas: No trip to Málaga would be complete without sampling espeto de sardinas, a dish that is as iconic to the city as the Mediterranean Sea itself. Fresh sardines are skewered and grilled over an open flame, usually on boats that line the beach, giving the fish a smoky, charred flavor. It's a simple yet deeply satisfying dish that speaks to the city's maritime roots. Visitors can find some of the best espeto de sardinas along the beach at El Palo, a neighborhood known for its chiringuitos, or beachside seafood shacks. Chiringuito El Tintero is a favorite among locals, where the staff famously auction off dishes to diners a fun and lively experience. Prices for *espeto de sardinas* range from €3 to €5, depending on the season. To get the best flavor, visit during the summer months when the sardines are at their freshest. The chiringuito is open from midday until late, with the best time to visit being just before sunset when you can enjoy the view of the sea while savoring this Málagan delicacy.

Rabo de Toro: For those craving something rich and hearty, rabo de toro, or oxtail stew, offers a deep dive into Andalusian comfort food. Originally a dish enjoyed by the working class after bullfights, it has evolved into one of the region's most beloved dishes. Slowly braised with wine, garlic, and vegetables until the meat is tender and flavorful, rabo de toro is a dish best enjoyed slowly, with a glass of local red wine. La Taberna del Pintxo, located in the vibrant area of Calle Larios, offers an outstanding version of this dish. The rustic setting, with traditional Andalusian tilework and warm lighting, provides the perfect backdrop for enjoying such a robust meal. Prices for rabo de toro start at €16, reflecting the time and care that goes into its preparation. The restaurant opens for lunch at 1:00 p.m. and remains open until midnight, making it a great choice for a late-night indulgence after a day of sightseeing.

Ajoblanco: One of Málaga's oldest and most distinctive dishes is ajoblanco, a chilled soup made from almonds, garlic, bread, olive oil, and sometimes grapes or melon for sweetness. The dish harks back to the city's Moorish heritage, offering a refreshing and slightly nutty flavor that is perfect for Málaga's warm climate. While it may be an acquired taste for some, it's a dish that provides a unique glimpse into the city's culinary evolution over the centuries. For the best ajoblanco, Casa Lola is a fantastic choice. Situated in the bustling center of Málaga, this charming eatery is known for its dedication to traditional Andalusian cuisine. Their *ajoblanco* is served beautifully, often with a few grapes for garnish, enhancing the balance of flavors. A bowl costs around €6, making it an affordable option for those looking to try something different. Casa Lola opens at 11:00 a.m. and closes at 1:00 a.m., making it an easy spot to drop by during the day or for a late-night snack.

Málaga's Cuisine: Málaga's culinary scene is a reflection of its rich history and cultural heritage. From the fishermen's humble gazpachuelo to the celebratory espeto de sardinas on the beach, each dish tells a story of the land and the people who have shaped this vibrant region. Visitors to Málaga will find that dining here is not just about the food, it's about connecting with the history, the flavors, and the soul of Andalusia. Whether you're sitting in a centuries-old bodega or a bustling beachside chiringuito, each bite is a step deeper into the heart of this enchanting city. The warmth of its people, the richness of its cuisine, and the beauty of its traditions make Málaga a true gastronomic treasure, inviting you to savor every moment.

6.3 Tapas and Wine Bars

Tapas and wine bars are at the heart of this culture, offering locals and visitors a delightful combination of small plates and quality wines. These establishments are more than just places to eat; they are social spaces where people come together to enjoy the art of Spanish dining. Below, we delve into the most distinctive tapas and wine bars in Málaga, each offering a unique experience, atmosphere, and selection of food and drinks.

El Tapeo de Cervantes: El Tapeo de Cervantes is a cozy and intimate tapas bar that has won the hearts of locals and visitors alike. Located just a few steps from the famous Teatro Cervantes, this gem is known for serving some of the most creative and flavorful tapas in the city. The menu is a vibrant blend of traditional Spanish dishes with a modern twist. Popular options include garlic prawns, tender grilled lamb, and their famous "berenjenas con miel" (eggplant with honey). The variety of dishes caters to both meat lovers and vegetarians, making it an inclusive dining spot. As for drinks, El Tapeo de Cervantes offers a well-curated selection of wines from across Spain, with an emphasis on Andalusian varieties. Prices are reasonable, with tapas ranging from €4 to €8 and wine by the glass starting at €3.50. The intimate space, with its charming, rustic décor, creates an inviting atmosphere where guests feel at home. It opens at 7:00 p.m. and stays open until midnight, making it an ideal spot for a late-night meal after exploring the city.

Vinería Cervantes: Just around the corner from El Tapeo de Cervantes is Vinería Cervantes, a sophisticated wine bar that pairs expertly selected wines with equally exquisite tapas. With its modern décor and sleek design, Vinería Cervantes attracts a more upscale crowd looking to savor Málaga's wine offerings. The wine list here is extensive, featuring not only local Andalusian wines but also bottles from Spain's premier wine regions, such as Rioja, Ribera del Duero, and Priorat. The food at Vinería Cervantes is just as impressive as the wine. Tapas include Iberian ham croquettes, seared tuna with soy sauce and sesame, and caramelized foie gras on toast. The flavors are bold yet balanced, and each dish is crafted to enhance the wine selection. Prices are slightly higher than at more casual spots, with tapas costing between €6 and €12, while wines by the glass range from €4 to €8. This wine bar opens at 1:00 p.m. and closes at 11:30 p.m., making it perfect for a late lunch or a refined evening of wine and tapas. Reservations are recommended, especially in the evening, as it tends to fill up quickly.

Bodega Bar El Pimpi: No visit to Málaga is complete without a stop at Bodega Bar El Pimpi. This legendary tapas and wine bar, located near the Alcazaba and Roman Theatre, is a cultural institution that has been serving locals and celebrities alike for decades. Stepping into El Pimpi feels like stepping into Málaga's past, with its traditional Andalusian décor, vast wine barrels signed by famous patrons, and a maze of rooms and terraces filled with laughter and conversation. The tapas menu at El Pimpi is rooted in local traditions, offering dishes such as fried anchovies, grilled sardines, and "porra antequerana" (a cold tomato-based soup similar to gazpacho). The bar also serves a variety of local wines, with the highlight being Málaga's sweet Moscatel wine, which pairs perfectly with their traditional dishes. Prices are moderate, with tapas starting at €4 and going up to €10, depending on the dish. Wines by the glass range from €3 to €7. El Pimpi opens its doors at noon and stays open until 1:00 a.m., making it a great spot for lunch, dinner, or a late-night drink. The outdoor terrace, with views of the Alcazaba, is particularly popular in the evenings.

Antigua Casa de Guardia: For a truly authentic experience, Antigua Casa de Guardia is a must-visit. Established in 1840, this historic wine bar is Málaga's oldest, and it has retained much of its old-world charm. Located on the bustling Alameda Principal, it offers a rustic, no-frills atmosphere that takes visitors back in time. Instead of modern seating, patrons stand at the bar as they sample wines poured directly from large wooden casks that line the walls. The focus here is on Málaga's traditional wines, particularly the city's famous sweet wines like Pedro Ximénez and Moscatel. Food is simple but delicious, with tapas consisting of olives, Iberian ham, and cured cheeses that complement the rich wines. Prices are very affordable, with wine by the glass costing as little as €2.50 and tapas priced between €3 and €7. Antigua Casa de Guardia opens early, at 10:00 a.m., and closes at 10:00 p.m., making it a perfect place to stop for a midday wine tasting or an early evening drink. The atmosphere is uniquely local, and visitors are sure to leave with a taste of Málaga's wine heritage.

La Tranca: Located in the trendy Soho district, La Tranca is a lively tapas bar that combines a love for traditional Spanish food with a fun, retro ambiance. The bar is decorated with vintage posters and old vinyl records, creating a unique atmosphere that is both nostalgic and modern. La Tranca is a popular spot among locals, known for its affordable tapas and bustling, energetic vibe. The menu at La Tranca is a celebration of classic tapas, including "ensaladilla rusa" (Russian salad), Spanish tortilla, and spicy chorizo. Their "montaditos" (small sandwiches) are also a favorite, offering fillings like Iberian ham, cheese, and marinated peppers. The drinks menu includes a range of Spanish wines, vermouth, and the ever-popular "rebujito" (a refreshing mix of sherry and soda). Prices are very budget-friendly, with most tapas costing between €2 and €6, and drinks starting at €2.50. La Tranca opens at 12:00 p.m. and stays open until 2:00 a.m., making it a great choice for both lunch and late-night tapas. The bar gets packed quickly, especially in the evenings, but the lively atmosphere and friendly service make the wait worth it.

6.4 Cooking Classes and Culinary Tours

A perfect way to immerse oneself in this world is through cooking classes and culinary tours, which provide hands-on experiences and deep insights into the local cuisine. These experiences allow visitors not only to taste Málaga's food but also to learn how to recreate it, understand its history, and appreciate the culture surrounding it. Here are standout cooking classes and culinary tours that offer a unique journey into the heart of Málaga's culinary landscape.

Spain Food Sherpas: Spain Food Sherpas is one of Málaga's most popular culinary experiences, offering both cooking classes and guided food tours. Located in the historic city center, this company gives visitors an insider's view of Málaga's food culture. Their signature experience starts with a guided tour through the bustling Mercado de Atarazanas, where participants explore the freshest local ingredients, including seafood, vegetables, meats, and spices. The market tour is a feast for the senses, with vibrant colors and rich aromas filling the air as the guide explains the importance of each ingredient in Andalusian cooking. After the market tour, guests participate in a hands-on cooking class where they learn to prepare traditional Spanish dishes such as paella, gazpacho, and Spanish tortilla. Wine is included in the experience, with local varieties offered to complement each dish. Prices for the combined market tour and cooking class are around €70 per person, and the experience lasts approximately four hours. Spain Food Sherpas operates daily, with morning classes starting at 10:00 a.m. and ending by 2:00 p.m. The small group sizes ensure a personalized experience, making it perfect for those looking to dive deep into the local culinary scene.

Cooking Málaga: For those seeking a more intimate and personal cooking experience, Cooking Málaga offers private classes with local chefs who invite participants into their own kitchens. Located in the charming Pedregalejo district, a short distance from the city center, this experience allows visitors to cook and dine in a relaxed, homey setting. The classes focus on authentic Andalusian dishes, with an emphasis on seafood due to Málaga's coastal location. Participants learn to prepare local specialties like "espeto de sardinas" (sardines skewered and grilled over an open flame) and "pescaito frito" (fried fish), along with typical side dishes like salads made with local ingredients. Cooking Málaga's private classes are available by appointment only, with flexible hours depending on the group's preference. Prices for a private class start at around €120 per person, which includes all ingredients, drinks, and a full meal. The personal attention provided by the chef makes this a unique and tailored experience, perfect for those who want to learn in a more relaxed, one-on-one environment. Classes typically last around three hours, with plenty of time to enjoy the fruits of your labor afterward.

Málaga Gourmet Tours: Málaga Gourmet Tours offers a comprehensive look at the city's culinary scene through guided walking tours that combine historical insights with food tastings. One of their most popular tours is the "Tapas and Wine Tour," which takes visitors through Málaga's winding streets, stopping at family-run taverns, wine bars, and hidden gems where locals dine. The tour focuses on traditional tapas paired with local wines, showcasing dishes like "porra antequerana" (a thicker version of gazpacho), "ensaladilla rusa" (Russian salad), and various seafood tapas. Along the way, participants learn about the history and significance of each dish and how it ties into Málaga's broader culinary traditions. The Tapas and Wine Tour is priced at approximately €60 per person and lasts three hours, with multiple tastings and drinks included. Málaga Gourmet Tours also offers private tours and can customize experiences for groups. Tours run daily, with start times ranging from 11:00 a.m. for lunch tours to 7:00 p.m. for dinner tours. This tour is ideal for those who prefer tasting their way through the city while gaining insight into the stories behind the food and the people who make it.

La Rosilla: For visitors who want to combine a love of food with the beauty of the Andalusian countryside, La Rosilla offers an unparalleled cooking experience in the Montes de Málaga, just a short drive from the city center. Set in a beautiful rural location, La Rosilla is a family-run business that provides cooking classes in a tranquil, picturesque setting. The experience begins with a tour of their organic garden, where participants learn about the importance of using fresh, local ingredients in Andalusian cooking. The cooking class itself covers a range of traditional Spanish dishes, with a focus on seasonal ingredients. Participants learn to prepare meals like "albondigas" (meatballs in almond sauce), "salmorejo" (a cold tomato and bread soup), and "ajo blanco" (a refreshing almond and garlic soup). After cooking, guests enjoy their meal on a terrace overlooking the stunning landscapes of the region, paired with local wines and homemade sangria. Prices start at €100 per person, and the experience lasts around five hours. La Rosilla offers classes by reservation only, with both morning and afternoon sessions available, making it a wonderful escape for food lovers who want to experience Málaga's rural charm.

Toma & Coe: Toma & Coe is a premium tour company that specializes in creating bespoke experiences for food enthusiasts in Málaga. Their private culinary tours are tailored to each client's preferences, making them ideal for those who want a personalized journey through the city's food culture. A typical Toma & Coe tour might include a visit to local markets, private tastings at family-run wineries, and cooking demonstrations by renowned chefs. The focus is on high-quality, artisanal ingredients, and participants often get exclusive access to some of Málaga's best-kept culinary secrets. One of the highlights of a Toma & Coe tour is the opportunity to visit small villages outside of Málaga, where traditional Andalusian cooking methods are still practiced. Here, visitors might learn to make homemade bread, "migas" (a traditional dish made from fried breadcrumbs), and "pisto" (a Spanish version of ratatouille), all while enjoying the scenic countryside. Prices for private tours vary depending on the itinerary but typically start at around €150 per person. Tours are available year-round, with flexible schedules to accommodate individual preferences. Toma & Coe offers a luxury culinary experience for those who want to delve deep into the gastronomic traditions of Málaga and Andalusia.

6.5 Local Markets and Street Food

The heart of Málaga's cuisine lies in the colorful local markets, where fresh ingredients abound, and the streets are filled with the aromas of freshly cooked food. The markets and street food vendors offer an authentic taste of Andalusian cuisine, and each has its own unique charm, showcasing the region's love for seafood, spices, fruits, and more. Visiting these markets and sampling the street food is an integral part of experiencing the city's true essence.

Mercado Central de Atarazanas: Mercado Central de Atarazanas is the city's largest and most famous market, and it is a must-visit for anyone who wants to experience Málaga's culinary culture. Located in the heart of the city, just a short walk from the historic center, this market is housed in a stunning 19th-century building that was once part of a shipyard, with the original Moorish gate still standing as its entrance. Inside, the market is a lively hub of activity, with vendors selling everything from fresh seafood and meats to fruits, vegetables, and spices. The food at Atarazanas reflects the bounty of the Mediterranean, with fresh fish like anchovies, sardines, and prawns available daily, as well as local fruits like pomegranates, figs, and citrus. One of the highlights of the market is the availability of ready-to-eat street food, where visitors can sample traditional dishes such as "boquerones fritos" (fried anchovies) and "calamares a la romana" (deep-fried calamari). Prices are reasonable, with tapas-sized portions starting at just €2. The market is open Monday to Saturday from 8:00 a.m. to 2:00 p.m., making it the perfect spot for a mid-morning snack or an early lunch.

El Mercado de la Merced: El Mercado de la Merced is a blend of tradition and modernity, located near the birthplace of Picasso in the vibrant Plaza de la Merced. This market has transformed from a traditional food market into a modern gastro-hub, where visitors can enjoy both traditional Andalusian fare and contemporary culinary innovations. Inside, there are stalls selling fresh produce and seafood, but the main draw is the array of food stalls offering street food and tapas from all over Spain. Visitors can try regional specialties like "ensaladilla rusa" (a Spanish version of potato salad), "croquetas" filled with jamón or cheese, and "pinchos morunos" (spiced grilled meat skewers). Prices for tapas range from €3 to €5, with larger portions available for those looking for a more substantial meal. The market also has a selection of local wines and craft beers, perfect for pairing with your food. El Mercado de la Merced is open from 10:00 a.m. to midnight, making it an excellent choice for both lunch and a lively evening out.

Mercado El Carmen: Tucked away in the neighborhood of El Perchel, Mercado El Carmen is a hidden gem for those who want to experience Málaga's seafood at its finest. This traditional market is much smaller than Atarazanas, but what it lacks in size, it makes up for in quality and authenticity. It's a favorite among locals who come here to buy fresh seafood caught in the nearby Mediterranean waters. The market is known for its selection of prawns, octopus, and mussels, all of which are sold at reasonable prices and can be cooked on the spot at one of the market's street food stalls. One of the standout dishes here is the "espetos de sardinas," a Málaga specialty where sardines are skewered and grilled over an open flame. This dish is a staple of Málaga's street food culture, and at Mercado El Carmen, you can enjoy it for just €3 per serving. The market is open Monday to Saturday from 8:00 a.m. to 2:00 p.m., and while it's primarily a morning market, there's a small bar inside that stays open into the afternoon, serving seafood tapas and local wines.

Street Food Along La Malagueta Beach: For those who prefer to combine Málaga's street food with a day at the beach, La Malagueta is the place to be. Stretching along the city's coastline, La Malagueta beach is not only known for its golden sands and clear waters but also for its abundance of "chiringuitos" (beachside food stalls). These stalls offer some of the best seafood street food in the city, with the salty sea breeze enhancing the flavors of the dishes. One of the most popular street food dishes at La Malagueta is "pescaito frito," a variety of small fish and seafood deep-fried to perfection. You'll also find "gambas a la plancha" (grilled prawns) and the ever-popular "espetos" (grilled sardines). Prices at the chiringuitos are higher than at the markets, with a plate of grilled sardines costing around €6 to €8, but the experience of eating fresh seafood right on the beach is worth every cent. The chiringuitos are open from lunchtime through the evening, making them a great option for a late afternoon snack or dinner while watching the sunset.

Mercado de Huelin: Located in the residential neighborhood of Huelin, just west of the city center, Mercado de Huelin is a local market that offers a more down-to-earth experience than the more touristy markets in the city center. This market is popular with locals who come to buy fresh produce, meats, and seafood, but it's also a great place to find delicious and affordable street food. The market is smaller and less crowded than Atarazanas, making it an ideal spot for those who want a quieter, more authentic experience. One of the market's unique features is its selection of "montaditos," small sandwiches filled with a variety of ingredients like jamón, chorizo, and fresh cheese. These montaditos are perfect for a quick snack and are priced at around €1 to €2 each. Another favorite is "empanadillas," Spanish-style turnovers filled with meat, tuna, or vegetables. The market is open Monday to Saturday from 8:00 a.m. to 2:30 p.m., and while it may not have the tourist appeal of the larger markets, it offers an authentic taste of everyday life in Málaga.

6.6 Nightlife and Flamenco Shows
Málaga is not just a city of sunny days and coastal beauty; when the sun sets, its nightlife awakens with a vibrant pulse that echoes through its historic streets. The combination of Andalusian passion, traditional flamenco, and modern nightlife creates an intoxicating atmosphere that invites visitors to experience the city in a completely different light. Whether you are drawn by the haunting sounds of a flamenco guitar or the energetic beat of a modern nightclub, Málaga's nightlife offers something for every soul, leaving an indelible mark on anyone who dares to explore it after dark.

Kelipe Centro de Arte Flamenco: For a truly authentic flamenco experience, Kelipe Centro de Arte Flamenco is the place to go. Tucked away in a quiet corner of Málaga's old town, this intimate venue focuses solely on the art of flamenco, offering a pure and unfiltered experience of this passionate Andalusian tradition. The performers at Kelipe are not just dancers and musicians; they are storytellers, channeling centuries of history, love, pain, and joy through their movements and melodies. The shows at Kelipe are intense and emotional, often leaving the audience breathless. With seating for only a small number of guests, the atmosphere is personal and immersive, making it feel as if you are part of the performance itself. Shows are held several times a week, with tickets priced at around €25, which includes a complimentary drink. Kelipe's dedication to preserving traditional flamenco makes it a must-visit for anyone seeking an evening of cultural immersion. The performances start at 9:00 p.m., and the magic lingers long after the last note fades.

Liceo Flamenco: In contrast to the rustic charm of other venues, Liceo Flamenco offers a more polished, contemporary flamenco experience. Located in a beautifully restored 19th-century mansion in the heart of Málaga, this venue blends tradition with elegance, making it a favorite for visitors looking for a refined evening out. The interior is sleek, with high ceilings, intricate architecture, and ambient lighting that sets the stage for a mesmerizing show. The performances at Liceo Flamenco are a blend of modern and traditional flamenco, with dancers pushing the boundaries of the art form while remaining rooted in its rich history. The combination of guitar, song, and dance is electrifying, with each performance leaving the audience in awe. Tickets are priced at €30, and the venue offers a selection of wines and tapas to enjoy during the show. The performances begin at 8:30 p.m. and last approximately 90 minutes, making Liceo Flamenco an ideal choice for an early night out or a prelude to further exploration of Málaga's nightlife.

Tablao Los Amayas: If you want to combine the beauty of Málaga's coastline with the excitement of a live flamenco show, Tablao Los Amayas is the perfect spot. Located just steps from La Malagueta Beach, this beachfront venue offers an unforgettable fusion of Andalusian tradition and seaside relaxation. The outdoor stage, with the sound of waves gently crashing in the background, adds a magical touch to the evening's entertainment. Los Amayas is known for its high-energy flamenco shows, featuring some of the best dancers and musicians in the region. The performances are lively and full of passion, making it impossible not to get caught up in the rhythm and emotion of the night. Shows start at 10:00 p.m., and tickets are priced at €25, which includes a drink. For those looking to enjoy dinner along with the show, the venue offers a selection of seafood dishes and traditional Andalusian fare, with prices ranging from €15 to €30. As the night goes on, the festive atmosphere often spills out onto the beach, where locals and visitors alike continue to celebrate Málaga's vibrant spirit.

Antigua Casa de Guardia: For a more relaxed and laid-back flamenco experience, Antigua Casa de Guardia offers a slice of old Málaga with a touch of flamenco flair. Established in 1840, this historic tavern is one of the oldest in the city, and it remains largely unchanged, with its long wooden bar, barrel-lined walls, and no-frills decor. Located near the port, this unpretentious venue is famous for its sweet Málaga wines, which are still served directly from the barrel. While Casa de Guardia is primarily a wine bar, it often hosts impromptu flamenco performances, where local musicians and dancers take to the small stage to entertain the crowd. The atmosphere is casual and convivial, with locals and tourists alike gathering to enjoy a glass of wine and the spontaneous rhythms of flamenco. Prices are affordable, with glasses of wine starting at just €1.50, making it an accessible option for those looking to experience Málaga's nightlife without breaking the bank. Casa de Guardia is open until midnight, and its relaxed vibe makes it a perfect spot to unwind after a day of exploring the city.

CHAPTER 7
DAY TRIPS AND EXCURSIONS

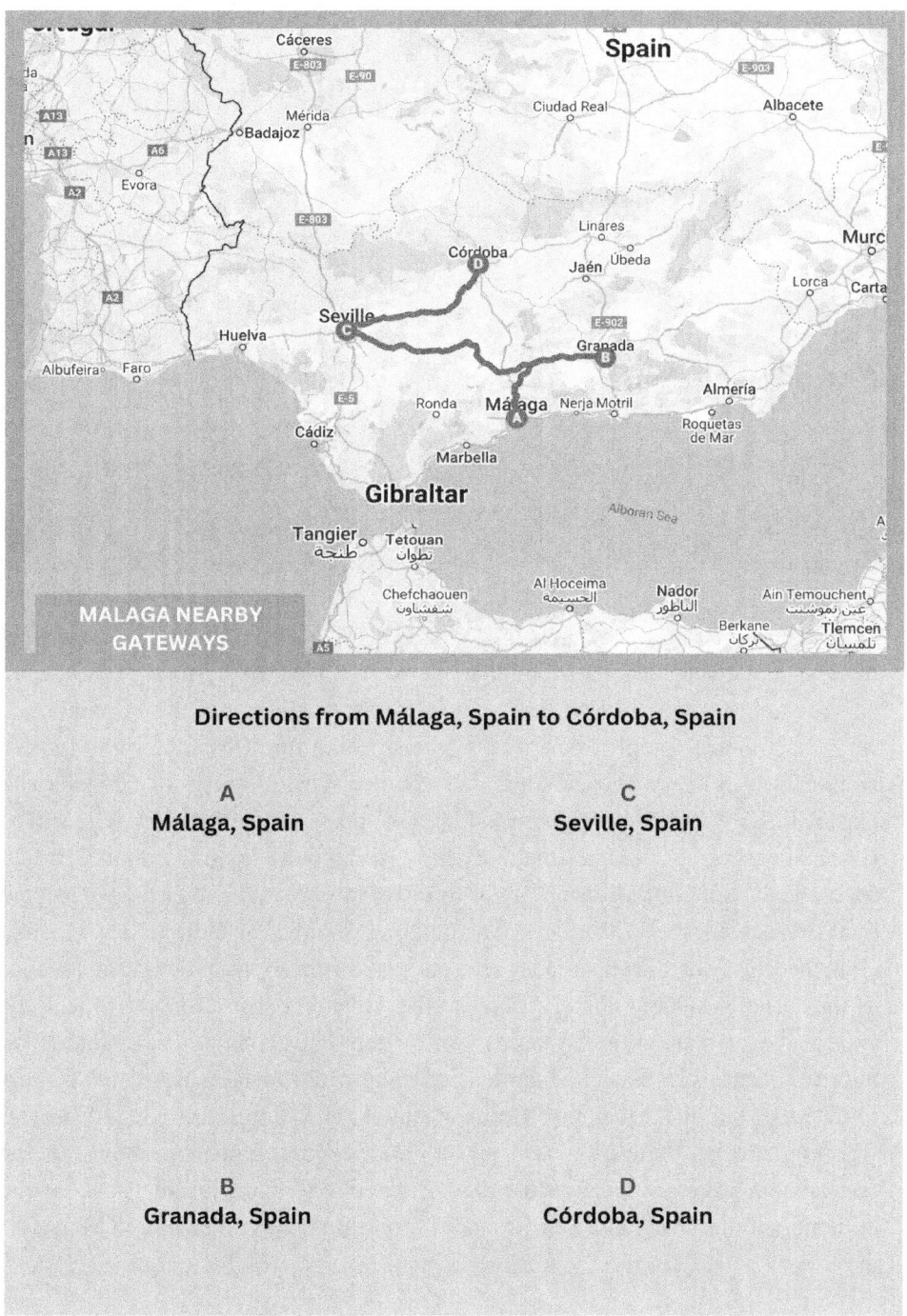

Directions from Málaga, Spain to Córdoba, Spain

A
Málaga, Spain

C
Seville, Spain

B
Granada, Spain

D
Córdoba, Spain

7.1 Granada

Granada, just 90 minutes by car or two hours by bus from Málaga, is a city that feels as though it belongs in another world. Situated at the foot of the Sierra Nevada mountains, this historic city is most famous for the Alhambra, a sprawling palace complex that stands as one of the finest examples of Moorish architecture in the world. Visitors who embark on a day trip to Granada can expect to be transported to a time of sultans, poets, and mysticism. The trip to Granada can be comfortably made by bus, with tickets costing around €10-€15 for a round trip. For those who prefer to travel in style and at their own pace, car rentals are available, with prices starting at approximately €30 per day. Once in Granada, the Alhambra is a must-see, but make sure to book tickets in advance as they tend to sell out quickly. Entry to the Alhambra costs around €14, and the experience of wandering through its intricately carved halls, courtyards filled with the scent of jasmine, and gardens adorned with fountains will leave visitors in awe. Beyond the Alhambra, Granada's old town is a treasure trove of narrow, winding streets, traditional tea houses, and vibrant flamenco shows in the Sacromonte caves. Expect a full day of discovery, from the elegance of the Alhambra to the lively pulse of Granada's nightlife before returning to Málaga.

Nerja and the Caves: Nerja, located about 50 kilometers east of Málaga, is a coastal gem known for its crystal-clear waters and dramatic cliffs. However, what truly sets Nerja apart is its famous caves, which stretch for nearly five kilometers and contain some of the world's most impressive stalactites and stalagmites. Day trips from Málaga to Nerja are easily accessible by bus, with tickets costing around €8-€10, or by car, with a scenic drive that takes just under an hour. The highlight of a trip to Nerja is undoubtedly the Cueva de Nerja, where visitors can explore vast caverns adorned with otherworldly formations. The caves also house prehistoric cave paintings, offering a glimpse into the lives of early humans who once called this region home. Entry to the caves costs around €10, and guided tours are available for those who want to dive deeper into the history and geology of the area. After exploring the caves, visitors can head to the Balcón de Europa, a stunning viewpoint that offers panoramic views of the Mediterranean Sea. Nerja's beaches, such as Playa de Burriana, are perfect for an afternoon of relaxation, and the town's seafood restaurants serve some of the freshest catches in the region. Expect to pay around €15-€25 for a delicious seafood meal by the sea, making Nerja a day trip that combines adventure with tranquility.

Caminito del Rey: For visitors seeking an adrenaline-pumping day trip, the Caminito del Rey is a thrilling experience. This famous walkway, suspended along the steep walls of the El Chorro Gorge, offers a unique way to explore the natural beauty of Málaga's inland landscape. Located about an hour's drive from the city, the Caminito del Rey can be reached by car or via a combination of train and shuttle bus, with transportation costs ranging from €10 to €15. The walkway itself is not for the faint of heart, as it traverses narrow paths and sheer cliffs, but the views are absolutely breathtaking. As visitors make their way along the route, they will be rewarded with panoramic vistas of the gorge, the Guadalhorce River, and the surrounding mountains. Tickets for the Caminito del Rey must be purchased in advance and cost around €10. The entire walk takes about three to four hours, making it a full-day adventure filled with excitement and awe. For those looking to wind down after the walk, nearby villages like Ardales offer charming spots to enjoy a meal or a drink, with traditional Andalusian dishes such as *porra antequerana* available for around €10. The Caminito del Rey is an unforgettable day trip that combines natural beauty with the thrill of adventure.

Antequera: A day trip to Antequera, often referred to as the "Heart of Andalusia," is a journey into the ancient past of the region. Located about 50 kilometers from Málaga, Antequera is home to some of Europe's most impressive prehistoric dolmens, as well as a stunning Moorish castle and a picturesque town center. Visitors can reach Antequera by bus for around €6 or drive through the rolling hills of Andalusia in about 45 minutes. The Dolmens of Antequera, a UNESCO World Heritage Site, are an extraordinary collection of prehistoric tombs that date back over 5,000 years. Walking through these ancient structures, visitors are transported to a time long before modern civilization, making it a deeply moving experience. Entrance to the dolmens is free, and guided tours are available for a small fee. Antequera itself is a charming town with a rich history, where visitors can explore the Alcazaba, a Moorish fortress that offers sweeping views of the surrounding countryside. For lunch, Antequera is known for its mollete, a soft bread roll that is often served with olive oil and jamón. Prices for a meal in Antequera range from €10 to €15, making it an affordable and delightful culinary stop. A day trip to Antequera offers a peaceful yet profound glimpse into Andalusia's deep history, from prehistoric times to the age of the Moors, making it a rewarding excursion from Málaga.

7.2 Seville

A day trip to Seville from Málaga is nothing short of a journey into the cultural soul of Andalusia. Located approximately 205 kilometers northwest of Málaga, Seville is accessible by both car and high-speed train. The AVE train is the fastest and most convenient option, whisking travelers to Seville in under two hours for around €45-€60 round trip. By car, the journey takes about two and a half hours, and while it offers scenic views of Andalusia's olive groves and rolling hills, the train is often the preferred choice for those wanting to maximize their time in Seville. Upon arrival in Seville, visitors are greeted by a city steeped in history, art, and passion. The magnificent Seville Cathedral, the largest Gothic cathedral in the world, dominates the skyline, with its famous Giralda Tower providing breathtaking views of the city. Just steps away, the Real Alcázar, a stunning palace complex blending Moorish and Renaissance architecture, offers a glimpse into the opulence of Spain's royal history. Wandering through the Alcázar's lush gardens is like stepping into a fairytale. No visit to Seville is complete without experiencing its vibrant local life. Seville's flamenco heritage runs deep, and visitors can end their day by attending an authentic flamenco show in the city's famed Triana district, where this passionate art form was born. After a day immersed in the rich culture and history of Seville, the return journey to Málaga allows travelers to reflect on the city's unforgettable sights and experiences.

Gibraltar: A day trip to Gibraltar offers an entirely different experience from the more traditional Andalusian excursions. Located about 135 kilometers southwest of Málaga, Gibraltar is a British overseas territory situated at the southern tip of Spain. The drive to Gibraltar takes just under two hours by car, and visitors should be prepared to cross an international border, so passports are essential. Gibraltar is famous for its dramatic Rock of Gibraltar, which rises majestically above the surrounding landscape. Visitors can take a cable car to the top of the Rock, where they'll be greeted by stunning views of the Mediterranean Sea and the coast of Africa on a clear day. The Rock is also home to a population of Barbary macaques, Europe's only wild monkeys, which are both playful and mischievous. Aside from the Rock, Gibraltar offers a unique blend of British and Spanish influences, from its red telephone boxes to its tapas bars. Visitors can explore the town center, where British-style pubs sit side by side with Andalusian restaurants, and enjoy duty-free shopping in this tax-free zone. A typical meal in Gibraltar costs around €15-€20, and the town's mix of cultures makes it a fascinating place to spend a day.

Mijas: For those seeking a more relaxed day trip filled with picturesque views and traditional Andalusian charm, Mijas is the perfect destination. Located just 35 kilometers from Málaga, Mijas is a short 40-minute drive or bus ride away, making it one of the most accessible excursions from the city. The village of Mijas is known for its whitewashed houses perched on the mountainside, offering stunning views of the Mediterranean coast below. Visitors to Mijas can explore the winding streets of the village, where local artisans sell handmade ceramics, leather goods, and other traditional crafts. One of Mijas' unique features is its famous donkey taxis, which have been a part of the village's charm for decades. While riding a donkey through the streets of Mijas may not be for everyone, it's certainly a quirky and memorable experience. Mijas also offers several viewpoints where visitors can take in panoramic vistas of the coastline, as well as the Ermita de la Virgen de la Peña, a small chapel carved into the rock that provides a peaceful retreat from the bustling village streets. For lunch, visitors can enjoy traditional Andalusian dishes such as gazpacho or paella at one of Mijas' many outdoor terraces, with prices ranging from €10 to €20.

Tarifa: For visitors who want to combine adventure with relaxation, a day trip to Tarifa is an excellent option. Located about 160 kilometers from Málaga, Tarifa is the southernmost point of mainland Spain and is renowned for its stunning beaches and strong winds, making it a popular destination for windsurfing and kitesurfing enthusiasts. The drive to Tarifa takes around two hours, and the scenic route along the coast provides beautiful views of the Mediterranean and the Atlantic. Upon arriving in Tarifa, visitors can explore the town's old quarter, with its narrow streets, Moorish architecture, and lively atmosphere. The main draw of Tarifa, however, is its beaches, where visitors can relax in the sun or take part in various water sports. Playa de Los Lances is the most popular beach for windsurfing, and equipment rentals and lessons are available for those who want to give it a try. Tarifa also offers ferry connections to Tangier in Morocco, so for the truly adventurous, a day trip across the Strait of Gibraltar to explore the markets and medinas of North Africa is a possibility, creating a truly unique experience.

7.3 Cordoba

A visit to Córdoba from Málaga offers an immersion into a world where Moorish architecture, Spanish history, and cultural richness blend seamlessly. Located around 160 kilometers from Málaga, Córdoba can be reached in just under an hour by the AVE high-speed train, with tickets ranging from €30 to €50 round trip. By car, the journey takes roughly an hour and a half, providing scenic views of the Andalusian countryside along the way. Córdoba's star attraction is undoubtedly the magnificent Mezquita-Catedral, a stunning mosque-cathedral that showcases the city's unique cultural legacy. Built in the 8th century as one of the grandest mosques of the Islamic world, it was later transformed into a cathedral following the Reconquista. The result is an awe-inspiring fusion of Moorish and Gothic architecture, with its endless rows of arches and intricate Islamic designs still intact. Visitors to the Mezquita can expect to pay around €11 for entry, and once inside, they'll be captivated by the beauty of the building's history, which speaks to the blending of faiths and cultures over the centuries. Outside the Mezquita, Córdoba's historic Jewish Quarter is a labyrinth of narrow cobblestone streets, lined with whitewashed houses adorned with flowers. The ancient Synagogue of Córdoba and the Alcázar de los Reyes Cristianos, with its stunning gardens and historic significance, are also must-visit spots for travelers eager to delve into the city's past. After a morning of exploring, visitors can enjoy a traditional Andalusian lunch at one of Córdoba's many local restaurants, with dishes like *salmorejo* and *rabo de toro* served for around €10-€15 per meal. The city's intimate patios, filled with flowers and fountains, provide the perfect setting for a relaxing afternoon.

Antequera: Located just 50 kilometers from Málaga, Antequera is an easy day trip for those interested in exploring the archaeological wonders and natural beauty of Andalusia. Known as "The Heart of Andalusia," Antequera is easily reached by car or train, with a journey time of just under an hour. Train tickets typically cost around €10-€15 each way, while the drive offers panoramic views of the olive groves and rolling hills that dominate the region. Antequera's most remarkable feature is its collection of prehistoric dolmens, ancient burial mounds that date back over 5,000 years. The Dolmen of Menga and the Dolmen of Viera are some of the largest and best-preserved megalithic structures in Europe, offering a fascinating glimpse into the region's ancient past. Just a short drive from the town, visitors can also explore El Torcal de Antequera, a nature reserve known for its surreal limestone rock formations. Hiking through El Torcal's otherworldly landscape, with its towering rocks and sweeping views, is an unforgettable experience for nature lovers and adventurers alike.

7.4 Ronda

Málaga, a vibrant coastal city basking in the Andalusian sun, serves as a gateway to numerous enchanting destinations that lie just beyond its shores. Among the most captivating of these is Ronda, a town perched high on the cliffs of the Serranía de Ronda, offering an extraordinary blend of dramatic landscapes, rich history, and cultural heritage. The journey from Málaga to Ronda unveils a tapestry of natural beauty and historical splendor, making it an unmissable day trip for anyone keen on experiencing the essence of southern Spain.

The Scenic Route to Ronda: The journey from Málaga to Ronda is a feast for the senses, beginning with the choice of transportation. Located approximately 100 kilometers from Málaga, Ronda can be reached by car, bus, or train. The drive from Málaga is a scenic adventure, taking about an hour and a half. As travelers leave the coastal plains behind, they ascend into the rugged terrain of the Serranía de Ronda, where rolling hills, olive groves, and vineyards create a picturesque backdrop. For those preferring public transport, regular buses depart from Málaga's central bus station, with a ticket costing around €12 each way. The bus journey, although slightly longer at approximately two hours, offers a comfortable ride through Andalusia's stunning countryside.

The Spectacle of Puente Nuevo: Upon arrival in Ronda, visitors are immediately struck by the town's most iconic landmark: the Puente Nuevo. This 18th-century bridge, which spans the El Tajo Gorge, is a masterpiece of engineering and one of Spain's most photographed structures. As visitors stand atop the bridge, they are treated to breathtaking views of the gorge's sheer cliffs and the river below. The Puente Nuevo's imposing architecture, with its three massive arches, creates a dramatic contrast against the natural landscape, providing an unforgettable photo opportunity.

Exploring Ronda's Historic Heart: Beyond the Puente Nuevo, Ronda's old town is a labyrinth of narrow streets, steep alleys, and charming squares, each offering a glimpse into the town's rich history. The Plaza de Toros, one of Spain's oldest bullrings, stands as a testament to Ronda's deep-rooted bullfighting traditions. Visitors can explore the bullring and its museum, gaining insights into the history and significance of bullfighting in Spanish culture. The museum's exhibits, including vintage posters and memorabilia, paint a vivid picture of this controversial and captivating sport. Nearby, the Mondragón Palace, a former Moorish residence turned museum, invites visitors to explore its beautifully restored interiors and lush gardens. The palace's architecture reflects Ronda's Islamic past, with intricate tilework and serene courtyards offering a tranquil retreat from the bustling streets.

The Natural Beauty of El Tajo Gorge: A visit to Ronda would be incomplete without venturing into the surrounding natural landscape. The El Tajo Gorge, carved by the Guadalevín River, offers stunning hiking opportunities. The trails along the gorge provide panoramic views of the town and its dramatic cliffs, making for a memorable outdoor adventure. Hikers can explore the rugged terrain, encounter diverse flora and fauna, and appreciate the unique geological formations that characterize the area.

Savoring Ronda's Culinary Delights: After a day of exploration, Ronda's dining scene provides a delightful conclusion to the visit. The town's restaurants offer a variety of traditional Andalusian dishes, with local specialties such as carillada (braised pork cheeks) and rabo de toro (oxtail stew) taking center stage. A typical meal costs between €15 and €25, with many restaurants featuring outdoor terraces that offer stunning views of the surrounding countryside. Dining in Ronda is not just about the food; it's also about the ambiance, with many establishments providing a cozy and authentic Andalusian experience.

CHAPTER 8
EVENTS AND FESTIVALS

8.1 Malaga Fair

Malaga comes alive in August with one of Spain's most vibrant and colorful celebrations. The Malaga Fair. Known locally as "Feria de Málaga," this annual event is a highlight of the summer season, attracting both locals and tourists from around the world. The fair is a week-long celebration of the city's history, culture, and traditions, offering a wide variety of events that take place throughout the city. The atmosphere during the fair is electric, with streets filled with music, dancing, and the joyful spirit of the Andalusian people. Held every August, usually in the middle of the month, the Malaga Fair pays homage to the city's historic liberation by the Catholic Monarchs, Ferdinand and Isabella, in 1487. This momentous event marked the return of Malaga to Christian rule, and the fair has since evolved into a week-long celebration of Andalusian culture, complete with flamenco performances, bullfights, and gastronomic delights. The fair is divided into two main areas: the "Feria de Día," held in the city center, and the "Feria de Noche," which takes place at the fairgrounds located just outside the city.

Feria de Día: The Feria de Día, or the Day Fair, is one of the most beloved aspects of the Malaga Fair. From midday until evening, the streets of Malaga's historic center come alive with music, dancing, and vibrant displays of Andalusian culture. The main areas for these festivities are Calle Larios, Plaza de la Constitución, and surrounding streets. These areas are beautifully decorated with colorful lights and banners, creating a festive atmosphere that is impossible to resist. Visitors to the Feria de Día can enjoy traditional flamenco performances, spontaneous street dancing, and live music performances at various plazas throughout the city. The air is filled with the sound of guitars, castanets, and the clapping of hands as both locals and tourists join in the festivities. One of the highlights is the presence of women dressed in traditional "trajes de flamenca," with bright, flowing dresses adorned with ruffles and polka dots. These women, along with men in traditional Andalusian attire, embody the spirit of the fair. For visitors wanting to experience local cuisine, the Feria de Día offers plenty of opportunities to indulge in tapas, seafood, and the famous "fino" sherry. Bars and restaurants set up stalls along the streets, serving everything from fried fish to plates of jamón ibérico, offering a true taste of Malaga's culinary traditions. To get to the city center, visitors can easily take public transportation such as buses or taxis, which are widely available during the fair. There is no entry fee to join the Feria de Día, making it accessible to everyone.

Feria de Noche: As the sun sets over Malaga, the fair transforms into a different kind of celebration known as the Feria de Noche. The heart of this night fair is located at the Real de la Feria, a large fairground just outside the city center in Cortijo de Torres. This area is easily accessible via public transportation, with shuttle buses running frequently from the city center to the fairgrounds. Entry to the fairgrounds is free, although rides, games, and certain performances may have individual fees. The Feria de Noche is famous for its thrilling amusement rides, illuminated by thousands of lights that create a magical atmosphere. Families can enjoy traditional carnival attractions, including Ferris wheels, roller coasters, and bumper cars, while food stalls offer churros, candy, and other fairground treats. For those looking for a more traditional experience, the fairgrounds also feature numerous "casetas"—private and public tents where visitors can dance the night away to live flamenco music and Sevillanas, a traditional Spanish folk dance. These casetas range from large public tents open to everyone, to more exclusive, private tents where members and their guests gather. One of the key features of the Feria de Noche is its diverse musical offerings. Visitors can find a mix of live performances ranging from flamenco to contemporary pop, ensuring there's something for everyone. The combination of traditional Andalusian culture and modern entertainment makes the Feria de Noche a must-visit for anyone looking to experience the spirit of Malaga after dark.

Romería: A deeply spiritual event that takes place during the Malaga Fair is the Romería, a religious pilgrimage that officially marks the beginning of the festivities. Held on the Saturday before the fair begins, the Romería honors the Virgen de la Victoria, the patron saint of Malaga. Participants, often dressed in traditional Andalusian attire, make their way on horseback, in horse-drawn carriages, or on foot from the city center to the Sanctuary of the Virgen de la Victoria, located just outside Malaga. The Romería is a touching tribute to the city's religious traditions, and the procession is filled with heartfelt devotion, music, and camaraderie. Along the way, participants sing traditional songs, play musical instruments, and offer prayers to the Virgin. The pilgrimage concludes with a mass at the sanctuary, followed by a day of celebrations and festivities. For visitors, this event offers a unique glimpse into the deep-rooted faith of the Malagueños and their commitment to preserving the traditions of their ancestors. To witness the Romería, visitors can head to the city center in the early morning, where the procession begins. Public transportation is available to the Sanctuary of the Virgen de la Victoria, or visitors can follow the procession on foot to experience the full spirit of the event. The Romería is free to attend, and it offers an enriching cultural experience for anyone interested in Spain's religious traditions.

Bullfighting at Plaza de Toros: For those looking to experience one of Spain's most controversial and iconic traditions, bullfighting is an integral part of the Malaga Fair. Held at the historic Plaza de Toros de La Malagueta, bullfights take place throughout the fair, drawing large crowds of both locals and tourists. The Plaza de Toros, located near the beachfront in La Malagueta, is easily accessible by public transportation, with buses and taxis readily available. The bullfights held during the Malaga Fair are part of the "Corrida Goyesca," a series of fights that feature some of the most renowned matadors in Spain. These events are steeped in tradition and are considered a significant part of Andalusian culture, dating back centuries. While bullfighting is not without controversy, many view it as an important cultural event that highlights the skill, bravery, and artistry of the matadors. Visitors interested in attending a bullfight can purchase tickets at the Plaza de Toros or online in advance. Prices vary depending on seating, with premium seats offering the best view of the action. For those unfamiliar with the customs of bullfighting, it is worth researching the event beforehand to fully understand its cultural significance. Despite the controversy, bullfighting remains a central element of the Malaga Fair, providing a glimpse into a tradition that has shaped Spanish identity for generations.

Flamenco Shows: No visit to the Malaga Fair would be complete without experiencing the passion and intensity of a flamenco show. Flamenco is the heart and soul of Andalusian culture, and during the fair, visitors can enjoy performances by some of the region's most talented artists. These performances take place throughout the city, with many bars, restaurants, and theaters offering special shows during the week of the fair. For a more intimate and authentic experience, visitors can head to one of the many "peñas flamencas," small clubs dedicated to preserving the art of flamenco. Here, guests can watch performances in a more traditional setting, often accompanied by a delicious meal and a glass of wine. These performances are emotionally charged, with dancers, singers, and musicians working together to create a powerful expression of Andalusian culture. Flamenco shows vary in price, with some venues offering free performances as part of the fair's festivities, while others charge for entry. Regardless of the cost, a flamenco show is an experience that should not be missed during the Malaga Fair, offering a deep connection to the region's artistic heritage.

8.2 Holy Week

Holy Week in Málaga, known as "Semana Santa," is one of the most extraordinary and intense religious events in Spain. Every year, the city comes alive with a deeply rooted tradition that combines faith, art, culture, and a unique Andalusian flair. Held during the month of April, this week-long celebration is a significant cultural experience for locals and visitors alike. Málaga's Holy Week is famous for its grandeur, emotions, and dedication, drawing thousands of people from around the world to witness the spectacle. The entire city transforms into an open-air theater of processions, traditions, and deep spiritual reflection. Here's a detailed look at key events during Holy Week in Málaga.

The Procession of El Cautivo: One of the most anticipated events of Málaga's Holy Week is the "Procesión de Nuestro Padre Jesús Cautivo," or the Procession of the Captive Jesus. This event takes place on Holy Monday and is held in the streets surrounding the historic center of Málaga. El Cautivo is particularly beloved by locals, and thousands gather to witness the majestic image of Christ as He is carried through the city, his hands tied and his gaze downward. To get there, you can easily reach the starting point at the Hospital Civil, near the city center, by walking from key landmarks or taking local buses. The procession usually begins at 8 p.m., and while there is no entry fee, arriving early is recommended to secure a good viewing spot along the procession route. What makes this procession truly special is the fervor it evokes among the crowd. The atmosphere is charged with emotion, and many devotees follow barefoot as a sign of devotion. The statue of El Cautivo is known for performing miracles, and many attendees have personal stories of answered prayers, adding to the profound spiritual meaning of this event. For visitors, it is not only a religious experience but also an opportunity to witness the deep-rooted devotion of the local community.

The Procession of La Paloma: The Procession of La Paloma, or the Dove, is another awe-inspiring event that takes place during Holy Week. Held on Holy Tuesday, it is considered one of the most beautiful and visually captivating processions. The Virgin Mary, depicted as La Paloma, is dressed in a white robe, symbolizing purity and peace, and her procession is adorned with thousands of white flowers. Starting from the Iglesia de San Juan, located in the heart of the city, this procession can be reached by walking from key locations like the Cathedral or taking a short bus ride from other parts of Málaga. No entry fees are required, but the streets fill quickly, so it's best to arrive early to find a good vantage point. The cultural significance of La Paloma lies in the image of the Virgin, who represents comfort and hope to many. The procession is known for its grace and the gentle music of the accompanying band, which plays traditional hymns that add to the serene atmosphere. This is a perfect event for visitors who wish to see the beauty and artistry of Holy Week in Málaga while reflecting on the themes of peace and love.

El Rico: The Procession of El Rico, held on Holy Wednesday, is a unique and deeply symbolic event that offers an experience unlike any other during Holy Week in Málaga. It is named after the figure of Nuestro Padre Jesús El Rico, who is carried through the city in a tradition dating back to the 18th century. During this procession, a prisoner is symbolically pardoned and set free, a ritual that signifies mercy and forgiveness. El Rico's procession starts at the Iglesia de

Santiago and winds its way through the city's narrow streets, filled with spectators. It is easily accessible from any part of Málaga's historic center by foot or public transportation. Like most of the Holy Week events, there is no admission fee, but the opportunity to witness the pardoning ceremony is priceless. The historical significance of this event dates back to the time of King Carlos III, who granted the brotherhood the right to pardon a prisoner every year. The act is performed in front of Málaga's City Hall, where the prisoner kneels before the statue of Christ and is granted freedom. Visitors attending this procession can expect a deep sense of emotion as they witness a centuries-old tradition that embodies themes of redemption and compassion.

La Expiración: On Holy Thursday, the streets of Málaga are filled with solemnity during the Procession of La Expiración. This event is known for its profound silence, which contrasts with the usual music-filled processions of the week. The central figure of this procession is Christ on the cross at the moment of expiration, surrounded by figures representing his followers and the Virgin Mary in mourning. The procession begins at the Iglesia de San Pedro, and you can easily reach it by walking or taking public transport. As with the other processions, no entry fees are required, but you should plan to arrive early to witness this moving event up close. The silence during La Expiración creates a unique atmosphere that is both solemn and reflective. For many, it offers a time for personal contemplation, and the visual impact of the statues, particularly the image of Christ at the moment of his death, leaves a lasting impression. Visitors will find this to be an introspective experience that invites them to connect with the deeper spiritual aspects of Holy Week in a way that few other events can.

The Procession of La Legión: On Good Friday, one of the most unique and powerful processions takes place: the Procession of La Legión, featuring the Christ of Good Death (Cristo de la Buena Muerte). What makes this event stand out is the participation of Spain's Legion, a military unit that honors Christ with a dramatic display of military precision and devotion. The soldiers carry the Christ of Good Death through the streets, and the crowd gathers in awe to watch the solemn procession. This event starts at the Iglesia de Santo Domingo and can be reached by walking from the main parts of the city or by taking public transportation. As with the other processions, no ticket is required, but finding a spot along the route can be challenging due to the massive crowds drawn to see La Legión. La Legión's participation adds a sense of military pride and unity to the religious celebration. The Christ of Good Death is the patron of the Spanish

Legion, and this procession reflects the deep bond between faith and military tradition in Spain. The synchronized steps of the soldiers, along with the grandeur of the statue, create an unforgettable spectacle that draws visitors from all over the world.

8.3 Malaga Film Festival

The Malaga Film Festival, held annually in the enchanting city of Malaga, has grown into one of Spain's most prestigious cinematic events. Taking place in March or April each year, this festival transforms the city into a lively hub of film, culture, and celebration. The festival's core mission is to promote Spanish-language cinema, fostering connections between filmmakers, industry professionals, and the public. The combination of warm spring weather, beautiful architecture, and the Mediterranean ambiance makes the festival an irresistible destination for cinephiles and culture enthusiasts alike.

The Opening Gala: The opening night of the Malaga Film Festival is nothing short of dazzling. The festival begins with a glamorous gala, usually held at the Teatro Cervantes, the city's iconic cultural landmark located in the historic center. Visitors can easily access the venue via public transport, with bus and metro lines stopping near the theater. The night marks the beginning of the festivities, filled with the arrival of film stars on the red carpet, press events, and the unveiling of the year's most anticipated films. Although the opening gala is by invitation only, the energy around the city during this event is palpable. Locals and tourists alike gather to watch the celebrities arrive, and the streets of Malaga buzz with excitement. For those interested in attending screenings, tickets for individual film viewings are available for purchase, typically costing around €10-15 depending on the venue and film. The opening night is significant as it sets the tone for the rest of the festival, symbolizing a celebration of cinema and the vibrant culture of Malaga. The event is worth visiting for its spectacle alone, but also for the opportunity to witness the beginning of a journey through the best of Spanish-language film.

Spanish Cinema Showcase: The heart of the Malaga Film Festival is its dedication to showcasing Spanish cinema. Films are screened across multiple venues, including the Teatro Cervantes, the Albéniz Cinema, and other cultural spaces in the city. These locations are easily accessible by foot if staying in central Malaga, or by bus and taxi if staying further afield. The screenings cover a wide range of genres, from dramas to comedies and documentaries, with a special emphasis on new directors and independent filmmakers. This platform allows both established filmmakers and emerging talent to share their work with an international audience. What makes this showcase truly special is the atmosphere of discovery. Visitors are treated to films that may never reach mainstream theaters, offering a unique window into Spanish-speaking cultures and stories. The screenings are often followed by Q&A sessions, giving visitors the chance to engage with the filmmakers directly, making the experience more personal and interactive. Tickets for these screenings are affordable, and attendees often find themselves mingling with actors, directors, and other film lovers in nearby cafés and bars, creating an intimate community vibe that resonates throughout the festival.

Masterclasses and Workshops: For those interested in the craft of filmmaking, the Malaga Film Festival offers a series of masterclasses and workshops conducted by industry professionals. These events are held throughout the city, often at venues like the Rectorado de la Universidad de Málaga or the CAC Málaga (Contemporary Art Center). Attending these sessions gives visitors an exclusive glimpse behind the scenes of the filmmaking process. The classes cover a variety of topics, including screenwriting, directing, cinematography, and acting, catering to both professionals and enthusiastic amateurs. Tickets for these workshops range in price, with some events being free of charge, particularly those geared toward students or aspiring filmmakers. The educational aspect of the festival adds depth to the visitor experience, allowing attendees to walk away not just entertained, but enriched with knowledge about the inner workings of cinema. Whether you're an industry professional or simply a fan of films, these workshops provide valuable insights and can deepen one's appreciation of the artistry involved in film production.

Awards Ceremony: The festival culminates in an elaborate awards ceremony that is another must-attend event. The closing gala, which takes place again at the grand Teatro Cervantes, is where the coveted awards are handed out. Categories include Best Film, Best Director, Best Actor/Actress, and more. The Golden Biznaga, the top award, is named after the iconic flower of Malaga, further grounding the festival in its local roots. This event draws prominent figures from the film industry, both from Spain and internationally, and has become a major media event covered by press outlets across the globe. Attending the awards ceremony requires an invitation, but visitors can enjoy the festivities in the surrounding streets where large screens broadcast the event, and crowds gather to cheer for their favorite films and stars. The ceremony is not only a celebration of cinema but a nod to Malaga's growing importance on the global film stage. The festival's cultural significance is immense, showcasing the city's dedication to supporting the arts and serving as a springboard for the careers of filmmakers.

Málaga in March: While the Malaga Film Festival is a major draw, the city itself is an attraction. Visitors should take advantage of their time in Malaga to explore its rich history and culture. From the ancient Roman theater and Moorish Alcazaba fortress to the renowned Picasso Museum, the city offers much to see and do between film screenings. The festival venues are mostly located within the city's historic district, so visitors can easily combine cinema with sightseeing. The local cuisine is another highlight, with numerous tapas bars and seaside restaurants offering delicious Andalusian dishes such as espetos (grilled sardines) and fresh seafood. During the festival, the entire city takes on a festive atmosphere, with special events such as concerts, street performances, and pop-up art exhibitions. Visitors can expect the streets to be lively, filled with music, dancing, and spontaneous gatherings celebrating the love of film and culture. The energy of the festival spills into every corner of the city, making it an unforgettable experience even for those who may not be attending all the screenings or galas.

8.4 Jazz Festival

Every November, the city of Malaga transforms into a haven for music lovers, as the Malaga Jazz Festival takes center stage. This internationally acclaimed event draws jazz enthusiasts from around the world, offering a diverse array of performances that span the entire spectrum of the genre. Held over several days, the festival is a must-attend for those seeking a blend of traditional and contemporary jazz, all set against the stunning backdrop of Malaga's historic venues. The festival, which has been running for over three decades, has become one of the most important jazz events in Spain, offering a dynamic blend of music, culture, and history.

The Main Stage at the Cervantes Theatre: The Cervantes Theatre, located in the heart of Malaga, serves as the primary venue for the Malaga Jazz Festival. This 19th-century theatre, with its grand architecture and impeccable acoustics, provides the perfect setting for some of the most highly anticipated performances during the festival. As the main stage, the Cervantes Theatre hosts internationally renowned jazz musicians, bands, and orchestras, showcasing everything from traditional swing and bebop to more experimental jazz sounds. The performances at the Cervantes Theatre typically take place in the evenings, and tickets are required for entry. Prices vary depending on the artist and seating arrangements, but most performances are reasonably priced, allowing both locals and visitors to enjoy world-class jazz in a historic setting. The theatre is easily accessible by public transportation, with bus routes stopping nearby and taxis readily available in the area. One of the reasons the main stage at the Cervantes Theatre is so special is its ability to transport the audience back in time. Sitting in the ornate seats of this beautifully preserved venue, you can feel the weight of history surrounding you as the music swells and fills the room. This combination of history and music makes attending a performance here a deeply enriching experience. For any jazz lover, a night at the Cervantes Theatre during the Malaga Jazz Festival is nothing short of magical.

Outdoor Jazz at Plaza de la Merced: For those who prefer a more casual and open-air experience, the Malaga Jazz Festival also hosts free outdoor performances in various public spaces, with Plaza de la Merced being one of the most popular locations. This vibrant square, located in the heart of the city, is not only a cultural hub but also the birthplace of Malaga's most famous artist, Pablo Picasso. During the festival, Plaza de la Merced comes alive with the sounds of jazz, as local and international artists perform on a stage set up in the middle of the square. These outdoor performances are free of charge, making them accessible to everyone, regardless of budget. The casual setting allows visitors to grab a seat at one of the many outdoor cafés surrounding the plaza, sip on a glass of wine, and enjoy the music in a relaxed atmosphere. The open-air concerts typically feature a wide range of jazz styles, from traditional New Orleans jazz to Latin jazz, and even modern fusion performances. This diversity ensures that there's something for every taste, whether you're a seasoned jazz aficionado or just discovering the genre for the first time. Getting to Plaza de la Merced is easy, as it is located in the city center and can be reached on foot from many of Malaga's main attractions. The nearby bus stops and taxi ranks also provide convenient access for those staying further away. The combination of beautiful weather, historic surroundings, and live jazz music makes these outdoor concerts a highlight of the festival, offering a unique way to experience Malaga's lively street culture while indulging in top-quality performances.

Late-Night Jam Sessions at The Clarence Jazz Club: The Malaga Jazz Festival is not just about formal concerts in grand venues; it also offers an opportunity for spontaneous creativity and intimate performances. One of the best places to experience this is The Clarence Jazz Club, a beloved venue among jazz enthusiasts in Malaga. Located in the Soho district, this cozy club hosts late-night jam sessions during the festival, where musicians come together to improvise and experiment with new sounds. These jam sessions are an essential part of the jazz tradition, where artists push the boundaries of the genre and engage in a musical dialogue that can be as thrilling for the audience as it is for the performers. At The Clarence Jazz Club, visitors can expect an intimate setting with dim lighting, excellent acoustics, and a warm, welcoming atmosphere. The venue is known for its laid-back vibe, allowing the audience to feel like they're part of the creative process as the musicians interact with one another on stage. The jam sessions typically start late in the evening and continue into the early hours of the morning, making it the perfect spot for night owls who want to keep the jazz experience going long after the main concerts have ended. There is usually a small cover charge for entry, and drinks are reasonably priced, adding to the relaxed atmosphere. Getting to The Clarence Jazz Club is easy, as it is located within walking distance of the city center, with taxis and buses readily available for those staying further afield. For visitors looking to experience the raw, spontaneous energy of jazz, these late-night sessions are a must.

Jazz at the Picasso Museum: The Picasso Museum, one of Malaga's most famous cultural landmarks, plays a special role during the Malaga Jazz Festival. As a tribute to the city's artistic heritage, the museum hosts a series of intimate jazz concerts in its beautiful courtyard. These concerts provide a unique fusion of art and music, as visitors can enjoy the sounds of jazz surrounded by the works of one of the 20th century's most influential artists. The concerts at the Picasso Museum are typically held in the afternoons, offering a more relaxed atmosphere compared to the evening performances at the theatre. Visitors can explore the museum's impressive collection of Picasso's works before settling into the courtyard for an afternoon of live jazz. The museum itself is located in the historic center of Malaga, making it easy to reach by foot or public transportation. Tickets for the jazz concerts at the Picasso Museum are usually sold separately from the museum's general admission, with prices varying depending on the artist performing. The setting, however, is well worth the cost, as the combination of world-class art and music creates an unforgettable experience. For visitors interested in both visual and auditory art forms, this event offers the perfect opportunity to indulge in both, making it one of the most unique aspects of the Malaga Jazz Festival.

Workshops and Masterclasses: In addition to the concerts and performances, the Malaga Jazz Festival also offers a range of workshops and masterclasses for those looking to deepen their understanding of jazz. These educational events are typically held at various venues around the city, including music schools and cultural centers, and are led by some of the festival's most prominent performers. Whether you're an aspiring musician or simply interested in learning more about the history and theory behind jazz, these workshops provide a hands-on, interactive experience. The workshops cover a wide range of topics, from the technical aspects of jazz performance to the cultural history of the genre. Some sessions focus on specific instruments, such as piano or saxophone, while others explore broader topics like improvisation and composition. For those attending, these workshops offer a rare opportunity to learn from world-class musicians in an intimate setting. The masterclasses often include live demonstrations, interactive Q&A sessions, and even the chance to perform alongside the instructors. The workshops and masterclasses are usually open to the public, with a nominal fee for participation. They are an excellent way for visitors to connect with the artists on a deeper level and gain a greater appreciation for the complexities of jazz music. Whether you're a musician looking to refine your skills or a curious listener wanting to know more about the art form, these educational events add an enriching dimension to the overall festival experience.

8.5 Christmas in Malaga

Christmas in Málaga is a dazzling celebration that combines centuries-old traditions with modern festivities, creating an unforgettable experience for locals and visitors alike. Held during the month of December, the city transforms into a winter wonderland, offering a rich variety of events that capture the magic of the season. From its famous light displays to festive markets and cultural performances, Málaga's Christmas celebrations invite visitors to immerse themselves in the spirit of joy and togetherness. Each event brings a unique charm and historical significance, making the holiday season in Málaga a truly special time.

The Spectacular Christmas Lights on Calle Larios: One of the most iconic events of Christmas in Málaga is the grand illumination of Calle Larios, the main shopping street in the city. Starting in late November and continuing throughout December, this light display is a must-see for anyone visiting during the festive season. The entire street is adorned with intricate designs of lights that create a tunnel of glowing beauty, often synchronized with music to enhance the visual experience. Located in the heart of the city, Calle Larios is easily accessible by foot from the historic center or by taking public transportation to the nearby Plaza de la Marina. There is no entry fee to enjoy the lights, and visitors can wander the street at their leisure, taking in the atmosphere of wonder and festivity. The significance of this event goes beyond its aesthetic appeal. The lighting ceremony marks the beginning of the Christmas season in Málaga and is eagerly awaited by locals who gather with friends and family to watch the first switch-on. For many, it's a nostalgic reminder of childhood Christmases, while for visitors, it offers a magical introduction to Málaga's holiday spirit. The lights on Calle Larios have become famous across Europe, drawing tourists from far and wide. Walking under these illuminated arches is not just about witnessing a beautiful display but feeling the joy and warmth that Christmas brings to the city.

The Nativity Scenes (Belenes): Throughout the Christmas season, Málaga is home to a number of intricate nativity scenes, or "Belenes," that are set up in churches, public spaces, and even private homes. These Belenes range from traditional displays to more elaborate representations, some of which include moving parts and detailed landscapes that tell the story of the birth of Christ. These displays can be seen throughout December and into early January. Key locations for viewing these nativity scenes include the Cathedral of Málaga, the Bishop's Palace, and the Museo Carmen Thyssen. Most of these displays are located in the historic center and can be easily reached on foot. Entry to view the Belenes is typically free, although some may request a small donation to support local charities. The Belenes hold a deep cultural and religious significance, as they represent the heart of the Christmas story for many Spanish families. Each scene is lovingly crafted, often by local artisans, and showcases a blend of faith, history, and creativity. Visiting the nativity scenes offers more than just an opportunity to admire the artistry; it allows visitors to connect with the spiritual essence of Christmas in Málaga. Whether you're religious or not, the beauty and care put into these displays evoke a sense of peace and reflection, making them a memorable part of any holiday visit.

The Málaga Christmas Market: Another highlight of Christmas in Málaga is the festive market, which takes place in Paseo del Parque, a picturesque tree-lined promenade located near the port. The market opens in early December and runs until the end of the holiday season, offering a vibrant mix of artisan crafts, handmade gifts, and traditional Spanish holiday treats. Visitors can reach the Christmas market by walking from the city center or taking a local bus that stops nearby. The market is free to enter, and you'll find plenty of stalls selling everything from handmade ornaments to leather goods, jewelry, and festive decorations. The Christmas market in Málaga is not only a great place to shop for unique gifts but also an opportunity to experience the local culture and holiday traditions. Vendors often sell delicious seasonal foods, such as "turrón" (a type of nougat), "polvorones" (crumbly almond cookies), and roasted chestnuts, which fill the air with the warm, comforting smells of Christmas. For visitors, this is a chance to mingle with locals, enjoy live music performances, and take part in the festive atmosphere that permeates the entire market. Whether you're looking for a special keepsake or simply want to soak in the holiday cheer, the Málaga Christmas market is a must-visit event.

Zambombas: One of the most unique and culturally rich events during Christmas in Málaga is the traditional Zambomba performances. Zambombas are folk music gatherings that have their roots in the Andalusian countryside, where groups of people come together to sing Christmas carols ("villancicos") accompanied by simple percussion instruments like the "zambomba," from which the event takes its name. Zambomba performances are held throughout December in various locations, including squares, bars, and community centers. Some of the most popular venues include Plaza de la Merced and Plaza de la Constitución, both of which are easily accessible from the historic center of Málaga. These performances are usually free to attend, but it's best to arrive early to secure a good spot, as they are often packed with locals eager to join in the singing and festivities. The cultural significance of the Zambomba lies in its communal spirit and its ability to bring people together through music. The songs, many of which are passed down through generations, reflect the joy and warmth of the holiday season, and the performances often turn into spontaneous parties where everyone is welcome to participate. For visitors, attending a Zambomba offers a chance to experience an authentic slice of Andalusian culture and to join in the fun by singing along or simply enjoying the lively atmosphere. It's a truly local experience that will leave you with fond memories of a uniquely Andalusian Christmas celebration.

The Three Kings Parade: The final event of the Christmas season in Málaga is the Three Kings Parade, held on the evening of January 5th. This grand parade, known as "Cabalgata de Reyes," celebrates the arrival of the Three Wise Men and marks the culmination of the Christmas holidays in Spain. The parade winds through the city streets, featuring elaborate floats, performers, and, of course, the Three Kings who throw candies and small gifts to the crowds. The parade starts at the Paseo del Parque and travels through key streets in the city center, making it easily accessible by foot or public transport. There is no fee to attend, but it's recommended to arrive early to find a good viewing spot along the route, as this event draws large crowds, particularly families with children. The Three Kings Parade holds great historical and cultural significance, as it represents the final celebration before the traditional Spanish gift-giving day on January 6th, known as "Día de Reyes" (Day of the Kings). For many children in Spain, this is the most anticipated day of the holiday season, as it's when they receive their Christmas presents. The parade itself is a visual feast, with colorful costumes, lively music, and a joyful atmosphere that spreads throughout the city.

INSIDER TIPS AND RECOMMENDATIONS

When it comes to exploring Malaga, there's much more than meets the eye. Beyond the bustling beaches and famous landmarks lies a wealth of hidden gems and experiences waiting to be uncovered by those in the know. As you plan your trip to this vibrant city on the Costa del Sol, here are some insider tips and recommendations to help you experience the true essence of Malaga. These are the secrets only seasoned travelers or locals would know, and they'll help you make your visit truly unforgettable.

Time Your Visit for the Best Experience: Malaga is an all-year-round destination, but if you're looking to avoid the crowds while still enjoying pleasant weather, the best time to visit is in the shoulder seasons – spring (April to early June) or autumn (September to October). During these months, you'll find fewer tourists and a more relaxed vibe, yet the weather is still perfect for exploring the city's streets or lounging by the beach. August is when Malaga hits its peak tourist season, and while it's exciting due to the famous Malaga Fair, be prepared for higher temperatures and busy streets. If you want a truly local experience, plan your trip around one of Malaga's unique cultural events, like the Holy Week processions (Semana Santa) or the August fair. Both are deeply rooted in the city's culture and offer visitors an incredible opportunity to witness tradition, community, and celebration in its most authentic form.

Wander Away From the Crowds: While places like the Alcazaba and the Picasso Museum are absolute must-sees, Malaga's charm truly shines in its lesser-known spots. For example, head to the district of El Palo, a traditional fishing neighborhood just a short bus ride from the city center. This is where you'll find the most authentic beach bars (chiringuitos) serving the famous espeto de sardinas – sardines skewered and grilled over an open flame. Here, you can enjoy a laid-back meal with your toes in the sand, far away from the more touristy beach areas. Another hidden gem is the Hammam Al Ándalus, tucked away in the historic center. This traditional Arab bathhouse is perfect for unwinding after a day of exploring. Few tourists know about this relaxing retreat, and it offers a tranquil oasis amidst the city's buzz, where you can indulge in soothing baths, massages, and beautiful Moorish architecture.

Discover Malaga's Rooftop Bars and Secret Views: One of the best ways to experience Malaga is from above. The city is full of rooftop bars offering spectacular views of the historic skyline, the Mediterranean Sea, and the surrounding mountains. For a romantic evening or a quiet escape from the busy streets below, make your way to one of these elevated spots. The rooftop of the AC Hotel Malaga Palacio is a favorite among locals. Here, you'll be treated to panoramic views of the harbor, the city's iconic cathedral, and the sea beyond. Arrive just before sunset to enjoy the golden hour light bathing the city in warm hues. Another hidden gem is the terrace at the Alcazaba Premium Hostel, where you can sip on cocktails while looking directly at the ancient Alcazaba fortress. If you're after a more adventurous view, hike up to the Gibralfaro Castle. Though not as frequented by tourists as the Alcazaba, the Gibralfaro offers some of the best vistas over the city, the port, and the sprawling coastline. The hike itself is a scenic journey, and the reward at the top is absolutely worth the effort.

Experience the Art and Culture Scene Like a Local: Malaga is a cultural hotspot, not only for its museums but also for its thriving local art scene. While many visitors flock to the Picasso Museum, true art lovers should take the time to explore Malaga's Soho neighborhood. Known as the "Barrio de las Artes" (the Arts District), Soho is filled with street art, independent galleries, and creative spaces that reflect the city's contemporary artistic pulse. One of the most exciting venues here is the Centre for Contemporary Art (CAC Malaga), which hosts a range of cutting-edge exhibitions and events featuring both local and international artists. For a more intimate experience with Malaga's creative culture, keep an eye out for local events like art openings, live music nights, or even poetry readings. The city's calendar is always filled with these kinds of low-key cultural happenings, many of which are free and attract locals more than tourists.

Dive into Local Gastronomy: No trip to Malaga would be complete without indulging in its rich culinary heritage. While tourists often flock to the more central restaurants, locals know that some of the best food can be found in the city's traditional markets. The Mercado de Atarazanas is a must-visit for any food lover. This bustling market is where you'll find fresh seafood, local produce, and traditional tapas. For a real insider experience, head here in the morning and join the locals for breakfast—try a freshly made "pitufo" sandwich (a small toasted roll) with tomato, olive oil, and a slice of jamón. Another insider tip: Don't leave without sampling "ajoblanco," a chilled almond and garlic soup that is a lesser-known but delicious Andalusian specialty. Pair it with a glass of local Málaga wine, and you'll truly feel like a local.

Embrace Malaga's Slow Pace: One of the most important tips for enjoying Malaga is to embrace its relaxed pace of life. The city is known for its easygoing atmosphere, so take the time to savor your experiences. Whether you're wandering through the narrow streets of the historic center, enjoying a long lunch in a sun-drenched plaza, or simply sitting on the beach watching the waves roll in, Malaga invites you to slow down and enjoy the moment. While sightseeing is undoubtedly important, the true essence of Malaga lies in soaking up its everyday rhythms. Sit at a café in the Plaza de la Constitución and watch the world go by, or spend an afternoon strolling along La Malagueta beach, enjoying the sound of the sea. The locals are proud of their city's laid-back vibe, and you'll find that taking the time to simply be present will make your trip all the more enriching.

Practical Tips for Navigating the City
While Malaga is a relatively easy city to navigate, a few insider tips can help you make the most of your visit. First, if you plan on using public transport, invest in a "bonobus," a multi-trip card that offers discounted rates on buses. This can be especially useful if you're staying outside the city center or plan on exploring neighborhoods like Pedregalejo or El Palo. For those who prefer walking, Malaga is incredibly pedestrian-friendly. Most of the main attractions are within walking distance of each other, and strolling through the city's historic streets is one of the best ways to discover its hidden corners. Wear comfortable shoes, as the cobblestone streets can be tricky, especially in the older parts of town.

By following these insider tips and recommendations, you'll be able to experience the city like a local, uncovering hidden gems and making memories that go beyond the typical tourist experience. Whether it's wandering through quiet neighborhoods, savoring authentic cuisine, or taking in breathtaking views from a rooftop bar, Malaga is a city that rewards curiosity and invites visitors to slow down and savor its unique blend of tradition and modernity. Your journey to Malaga will be one filled with unexpected discoveries, and once you've experienced its warmth and beauty, you'll find yourself longing to return again and again.

Printed in Great Britain
by Amazon